# Bums on Seats

A comedy

# Michael Snelgrove

Samuel French — London
New York - Toronto - Hollywood

# BUMS ON SEATS

A slightly shortened version of this script was first presented
by the Backstage Theatre Company at South Hill Park
Arts Centre, Bracknell, on 18th July 1995. It then opened
with the following cast at Adam House Theatre as part of
the Edinburgh Fringe Festival on 14th August 1995,
produced by the Backstage Theatre Company in
association with South Hill Park Arts Centre:

| | |
|---|---|
| **Petronella** | Gerri McGhee |
| **Felicity** | Patsy Golding |
| **Jacintha** | Franca Megaro |
| **Wendy** | Dawn Morris |
| **Estelle Nettlebank** | Jenny Hooper |
| **Mo/Tanya Steele** | Jane Shone |
| **Benedict Thrush** | Leigh Symonds |
| **Hugo Gelt/Lionel Heap** | Jerry Radburn |
| **Zara Roscoff/June Heap** | Robbie Pettitt |
| **Roland Luckett/Werner Meister** | Phil Lewis |
| **Alan Bland** | Chris Pettitt |
| **Gerald Bliss Hart** | David Edwards |

Directed by Mike Snelgrove
Set designer  Sue Lawson Dick
Set construction  Ken Gillard and Don Lucas
Lighting designer  Martin Kempton
Costumes  Amanda Pennington
Produced by David Edwards

NB The roles of Felicity and Alan Bland have been
removed from this published version of the script.

# CHARACTERS

**Wendy**, usherette; any age
**Petronella**, usherette; any age
**Jacintha**, usherette; any age
**Estelle Nettlebank**, Marketing Assistant; 20s-30s
**Mo**, stage manager; 30s
**Benedict Thrush**, actor; 20s
**Zara**, actress; any age
**Hugo**, actor; any age
**Roland Luckett**, author; 50s
**Werner Meister**, actor; 60s
**Tanya**, sponsor; 30s
**Lionel Heap**, local Labour politician; 40s
**June Heap**, Lionel's wife; 40s
**Gerald Bliss Hart**, local Conservative politician; 50s
**Marcia Bliss Hart**, Gerald's wife; 40s
**Aaron Zoffany**; any age

The action of the play takes place on the stage, then in the auditorium, of a provincial theatre

Time: the present

# AUTHOR'S NOTE
## Doubling

Although *Bums on Seats* can be performed with each part played by a single actor, the doubling of roles can make the production more interesting and challenging for both cast and audience. It's also more economical! Casting in the original productions varied because of different circumstances, but the best combination turned out to be:

Actor 1 plays **Hugo Gelt** and **Lionel Heap**
Actor 2 plays **Benedict Thrush** and **Gerald Bliss Hart**
Actor 3 plays **Roland Luckett** and **Werner Meister**
Actress 1 plays **Zara Roscoff** and **June Heap**
Actress 2 plays **Estelle Nettlebank**
Actress 3 plays **Mo** and **Tanya Steele**
Actress 4 plays **Petronella** and **Marcia Bliss Hart**
Actress 5 plays **Jacintha** and **Aaron Zoffany the Third**
Actress 6 plays **Wendy**

This play is dedicated to:
David Edwards,
the Backstage Theatre Company
and *The Running Horse*, Bracknell,
without whom ...

*Other plays by Michael Snelgrove published by*
*Samuel French Ltd*

Definitely Eric Geddis
Hidden Meanings
Maurice (Dancing)
Sleep Tight Tonight
Urban Cycles

# ACT I

*The stage of a more-than-slightly run-down theatre in the provinces*

*The stage is set for a performance of a new play called "Fecund". "Fecund" is set in the delivery room of a hospital's maternity wing. The set designer has obviously had a literal and metaphorical rush of blood to the head: the walls and floor are covered in blood and the set is dominated by a huge operating table, covered by a white but bloodied sheet. The set designer has also painted the floor and walls with abstract designs reflecting the symbolism of the piece: the overall effect is of a psychopath run mad with a chainsaw in a morgue*

*There are seats to one side of the stage for the usherettes, also a notice-board or screen for the display or projection of captions, controlled from onstage*

*When the play begins, the stage and auditorium are in semi-darkness. Under the sheet lies Mo, motionless*

*Wendy, an usherette, enters with a torch. She dramatically places it underneath her chin and switches it on. Nothing. The batteries are evidently flat. She shakes the torch about*

*Petronella and Jacintha, the other usherettes, enter with torches. They are both resting actresses. They move dramatically, eventually striking somewhat over-dramatic postures*

*Wendy looks rather confused by the routine*

*The Lights come up on the stage during the following*

**Petronella** Stop.
**Jacintha** Breathe.
**Petronella** Centre.
**Jacintha** Focus.
**Wendy** Ummmm ...
**Petronella** ⎱ (*together*) Ssssh!
**Jacintha** ⎰
**Jacintha** Focus! And ...
**Petronella** Release.

*Petronella and Jacintha exhale, dramatically*

   God, I love it!
**Jacintha**  Being in the theatre.
**Petronella**  *Being* in the theatre. The release of energy ...
**Jacintha**  Physical.
**Petronella**  And emotional.
**Jacintha**  It's like — an orgasm!
**Wendy**  Language ...

*Petronella and Jacintha look at Wendy. She smiles weakly*

**Petronella**  Look at it. The peeling paint.
**Jacintha**  The fading gilt.
**Petronella**  The musty plush.
**Jacintha**  The hole in the carpet.
**Petronella**  The tear in the seat.
**Petronella**
**Jacintha**  } (*together*) The magic of the theatre!

*Wendy looks unconvinced. There is a pause. Petronella and Jacintha look at Wendy*

**Wendy**  Oh, absolutely.
**Jacintha**  Cast list.
**Petronella**  Petronella.
**Jacintha**  Jacintha.
**Wendy**  Wendy.
**Petronella**
**Jacintha**  } (*together*) AKA.
**Jacintha**  Everyone has a nickname in the business.
**Petronella**  Pet.
**Jacintha**  Jack.
**Wendy**  Wendy.
**Petronella**  Don't be deceived. This isn't what we do.
**Jacintha**  Only a stopgap, this.
**Petronella**  We're in the business.
**Jacintha**  Couldn't be anywhere else.
**Petronella**  We live it.
**Jacintha**  Breathe it.
**Petronella**  Eat it.
**Jacintha**  Other actors.
**Petronella**
**Jacintha**  } (*together*) Bless!

**Jacintha** Warm, open, generous human beings. Brave ——
**Petronella** You have to be.
**Jacintha** To stand up there on a stage, naked ——
**Wendy** Emotionally speaking.
**Petronella** To expose yourself ——
**Wendy** Spiritually, we mean.
**Petronella** — to total strangers.
**Jacintha** All for you — yes, you! The glorious, wonderful many-headed ——
**Wendy** Sparsely-headed at matinées ——
**Jacintha** — monster — the audience!
**Petronella** ⎱
**Jacintha** ⎰ (*together*) It's a brave, lonely, rather wonderful life.
**Wendy** Being in the audience?
**Petronella** Being in the profession.
**Jacintha** Bless. Of course, it makes us terribly insecure.
**Petronella** It's why we kiss all the time.
**Jacintha** It's why we touch.
**Wendy** I don't much like the touching.
**Petronella** We're a very touchy profession.
**Wendy** Especially in the dressing room.
**Petronella** ⎱ (*together*) Huggy-huggy, touchy-touchy, feely-feely, kissy-
**Jacintha** ⎰          kissy. Bless. Love.

*Pause*

**Wendy** We're unemployed.
**Petronella** ⎱
**Jacintha** ⎰ (*together, outraged*) We're resting!
**Jacintha** And even when we're resting, we're working.
**Petronella** Selling programmes.
**Jacintha** Tearing tickets.
**Petronella** Dispensing ice-creams.
**Wendy** Attending toilets.
**Petronella** Everything, after all, is performance. Even the picking up of a
   giro can be an act of theatre.
**Jacintha** A weekly matinée.
**Petronella** A tragedy.
**Wendy** A farce.
**Jacintha** Love.
**Petronella** Bless.
**Jacintha** The government's fault, of course.
**Petronella** Philistines.
**Jacintha** We're not valued. And it's not as though we're not professionals.
   We've trained.
**Petronella** My God, we've trained!

**Jacintha**  RADA and Central.
**Petronella**  Guildhall.
**Wendy**  Guildford.
**Petronella** ⎫
**Jacintha** ⎭ (*together*) But nobody *understands* ...
**Petronella**  So, we'll show you.

*Petronella and Jacintha indicate that Wendy should display a caption at the side of the stage, which she does. It reads: "9.40 a.m. Just Follow Me"*

**Jacintha**  Nine forty a.m.
**Petronella**  For those of you with reading difficulties.
**Petronella** ⎫
**Jacintha** ⎭ (*together*) Love.
**Jacintha**  *Just Follow Me.*
**Wendy**  Is that what they call an alienation device?
**Petronella** ⎫
**Jacintha** ⎭ (*together*) Bless.

*There is a lighting change*

   *The usherettes disappear*

*The Lights fade so we are back in the semi-lit state of the beginning of the play*

**Estelle** (*off*)  Just follow me. That's right. Just follow me.

*Estelle appears, in a hurry. She is in her late twenties or early thirties. She is smartly, perhaps slightly theatrically, dressed in a suit with accessories. She has an untidy sheaf of papers in her hand and the odd strand of hair escapes from its captivity. She consults her notes*

Now ... if you'd all like just to gather on the ... (*she consults her notes*) ... the stage. (*She closes her eyes to learn the phrase*) The stage, the stage, the ... That's right. Just move into any space you can find. Just follow each other. (*She motions to an invisible group of people, waving them along, smiling unnaturally at them*) Well, welcome, everybody to our tour of the Theatre Royal. (*She looks at different groups of imaginary tourists in turn*) Bonjour. Guten Morgen. Hi y'all. And whatever the Japanese is. Where better to begin our tour than on the ... (*another check of the notes*) ... stage of the Theatre Royal itself? (*She looks at her watch*) By the end of our tour, you will see that putting on a play involves a lot more than a few actors knowing their lines and not bumping into the furniture, as Noël Coward — the Master, as we call him still — once so memorably quipped. (*Under her breath*) My God, what were you on when you wrote this, Estelle? In the best traditions of the theatre, it goes without saying that the Theatre Royal has its very own ghost. A white shrouded, terrifying figure ——

*The figure on the delivery table — Mo — jerks up to a sitting position and sits there, unmoving*

— who appears ...

*Mo moans loudly. Estelle screams and jumps about twelve feet into the air. The figure wrestles with the sheet and eventually manages to pull it off to reveal herself. She is probably in her mid-thirties but her spiky punk gear and warpaint makes it hard to tell. She is suffering from a massive hangover. Far from reassuring her, Mo's real appearance only heightens Estelle's concern*

**Estelle** Avaunt, and quit my sight! (*She continues to scream under Mo's next line*)
**Mo** Oh, my bloody head! Look, just shut up, will you? Right? You're doing my head in!

*Estelle quietens down a bit*

Where the hell am I? (*She pulls down the sheet to reveal a very bloodied baby doll sitting between her legs staring up at her*) Oh, no. Not *again*. Not months of puking and sore nipples. Not again. Nurse, nip out and get me a large coffee and a packet of Marlboro Lights, will you, there's a darling?
**Estelle** I'm not a nurse. I'm Estelle Nettlebank. Marketing.
**Mo** Right. Hold on. God, my mouth's like the Nevada desert after a nuclear test.

*Mo climbs off the table and disappears through one of the exits*

*There is a clunk offstage and the working lights come on, rather startling Estelle*

*After a few moments, Mo reappears, rather miraculously, with a polystyrene cup of coffee and a cigarette. She takes a drag on her cigarette and a deep draught of coffee and starts to look better*

**Mo** That's better. Like what was all that screaming about?
**Estelle** You startled me.
**Mo** I startled *you*? Right! (*She laughs rather bitterly*)

**Estelle** I thought you were ...

**Mo** What?

**Estelle** Nothing.

**Mo** You new?

**Estelle** I started last week.

**Mo** Hard cheese.

**Estelle** And you're ... ?

**Mo** Mo. Chief Stage Manager. Listen, have I been home, do you know?

**Estelle** I don't think you have.

**Mo** Oh, God. She'll go mad. Well, tough, right? So I went to the first night party, so what? And I came out here to have a lie down, right? Because my head was going round. Next thing I know I'm having a dream about having a group session with Judith Chalmers and the entire *Wish You Were Here* team. Weird. Did you catch it last night?

**Estelle** I didn't catch anything last night.

**Mo** The show, love. The show.

**Estelle** ""Fecund"?

**Mo** "Fecund".

**Estelle** Yes. No. It was my badminton night.

**Mo** "Fecund". Bloody stupid title. Know what it means?

**Estelle** (*thinking*) No.

**Mo** Nor do I.

**Estelle** It's one of those words, isn't it?

**Mo** Right.

**Estelle** (*indicating the blood-soaked walls*) Did somebody get killed?

**Mo** Right, yeah! (*She laughs and winces*) No. This is the set, right? Rumour has it it's supposed to be, like, the delivery room in a maternity hospital. So I said to the designer, at least I assumed he was the designer — jaunty little cap, single ear-ring, pocketed his fee and pissed off back to London — I said to him, I said, "Listen, I've had five children — in the days when I was into all that sort of thing — and I've never seen a delivery room like this." And, like, he goes it was a concept, right? Listen, when you hear the word "concept" in the theatre, you know you're in deep shit, yeah? So, right, don't take any of it too seriously if you don't want your head done in.

**Estelle** (*disapprovingly*) That doesn't sound very professional.

**Mo** I'm going to have to make a phone call. Listen, it's only, like, a play, love, yeah? There'll be another one along in three weeks' time. Like a privatized rural train service ...

*Mo leaves, using a door other than that used by Estelle*

*Estelle hangs around for a moment, uncertain what to do. She shrugs and gives a little giggle*

**Estelle** Oh, well. (*She sings, not very well*) No business like ... Where was
I? Oh, yes. (*She clears her throat, takes up a stance and continues*) ... learn
your lines and don't bump into the furniture, as ——

*A door slams, off*

*Benedict appears. He is a young actor in his early twenties. He dresses in
the apparently rough but actually minutely considered gear of the young
acting turk*

**Benedict** (*looking back to the door*) Shit.
**Estelle** Oh.
**Benedict** Shit, shit, shit. (*He sees Estelle*) Sorry. I didn't mean to ...
**Estelle** No, no. I was only ——
**Benedict** It's just some people, you know? Some people, they're just so ...
I mean, my head's like a pressure cooker sometimes. And do you know
what she did?
**Estelle** No.
**Benedict** She only got in the same taxi as me! I mean, that's off. That is
definitely off. I mean, what if her old man had ... I mean, that was no part
of our arrangement, our ... sorry ...
**Estelle** No, no ...
**Benedict** I just felt I had to get that off my chest ...
**Estelle** Yes, yes.
**Benedict** I'm interrupting you.
**Estelle** Yes. No.
**Benedict** It's just sometimes the stage is the only place, you know?
**Estelle** Yes. No. I've got no idea what you're talking about, actually.
**Benedict** The only place where I can feel real. (*He laughs, hollowly*)

*Estelle bemusedly joins in with the laughter*

God, that says something, doesn't it? The only place I can be in touch with
reality is the place of ultimate illusion and deception.
**Estelle** It does seem slightly ——
**Benedict** Look, I'm stopping you.
**Estelle** No.
**Benedict** You rehearsing?
**Estelle** Yes.
**Benedict** Anything interesting?
**Estelle** No. Well ——
**Benedict** Right. I mean, it's like this thing that I'm in. I know, I *know* that
I haven't got it. I know it's there somewhere and if I can just ... but it's just
always that bit out of my grasp, you know?

**Estelle** This is "Fecund"?

**Benedict** Right. Interesting piece. Very interesting.

**Estelle** I haven't managed to see it yet. What does it mean?

**Benedict** Well, this is it. This is what I'm saying. If I could ... you know?
If I could just get inside the man's head, strip away the camouflage
and ——

**Estelle** No. The word. Fecund. What does it mean?

**Benedict** Umm ... (*He thinks intensely*) No idea.

**Estelle** It's one of those words, isn't it?

**Benedict** Right. What words?

**Estelle** One of those words you think you know the meaning of, but when
you come to think about it ...

**Benedict** I'll ask Roland.

**Estelle** He'll know, will he?

**Benedict** Shouldn't think so. He's the playwright.

*Estelle smiles*

(*Relaxing a bit*) What are you rehearsing?

**Estelle** The Guided Tour.

**Benedict** Don't know it. Sounds interesting. New piece?

**Estelle** No. Yes, I suppose. I ——

**Benedict** European, is it? German, I'll bet.

**Estelle** I wrote it last night.

**Benedict** You wrote it?

**Estelle** Yes.

**Benedict** You wrote a play in one night? Eat your heart out Alan "Bash-Out-
A-Play-In-Ten-Minutes-Flat" Ayckbourn!

**Estelle** It's not a play. It's the guided tour, really. I work in Marketing. I'm
the new Marketing Assistant. And today's the first day I give the guided
tour. Of the theatre. I was just practising.

**Benedict** Rehearsing. Right.

**Estelle** Estelle Nettlebank.

**Benedict** Benedict Thrush.

**Estelle** You're an actor.

**Benedict** How did you know?

*Estelle shrugs*

Sometimes I'm an actor. Sometimes I just stand there and say the words.
Those are the days when I go home feeling ashamed. Physically and
emotionally ashamed.

**Estelle** Actually, I've seen you on TV.

**Benedict**  Oh. That. Those are the days when I crawl home feeling sub-
human.

**Estelle**  It's very funny.

*Benedict snorts*

Well ... for a sitcom.

**Benedict**  So what about you? You're in Marketing, yes? Interesting.
Interesting.

**Estelle**  That's what I do now, but ...

**Benedict**  (*looking worriedly out of the door, not listening*)  Interesting,
interesting.

**Estelle**  I've only been here a few weeks. I came here from British Rail. And
what's more I was very nearly on time.

**Benedict**  Sorry?

**Estelle**  Don't laugh. I was Public Relations Officer for the Network South
East Mobile Catering Display Team.

**Benedict**  That must have been really ...

**Estelle**  Interesting? Yes, it was, quite. It had its moments. Well, breakfast,
lunch, tea and dinner, to be precise.

**Benedict**  Sorry?

**Estelle**  We never had to do guided tours at Network South East. The last thing
we wanted the public to see was what really went on.

**Benedict**  Look, I know. I've had an idea. I've just had a really great idea.
Why don't you do it for me?

**Estelle**  What?

**Benedict**  Just, you know, do it. For me. I'll watch. I'll listen.

**Estelle**  That's very kind of you, but, really ——

**Benedict**  Listen, I've just had another really great idea.

**Estelle**  Oh.

**Benedict**  I'll be one of your tourists.

**Estelle**  What?

**Benedict**  Role play. Simulation. Give you the feel.

**Estelle**  I don't know.

**Benedict**  Trust me. I'm a professional.

**Estelle**  All right. (*She clears her throat, glances at her notes*)

*During the following, Benedict goes through an elaborate, silent warm-up
routine*

Welcome to the Theatre Royal. An historic theatre has stood on this site
since 1958, when the Mayor, Alderman Mr Whitworth ——

**Benedict**  Stop. Sorry. Do you mind?

**Estelle** What?

**Benedict** Sorry. I'm not ready.

**Estelle** You're not ready?

**Benedict** I'm not sure about this guy. This man.

**Estelle** Alderman Whitworth?

**Benedict** Who? No. This man. My man. I've got nothing to hold on to, no — image. No feel.

**Estelle** Is it important? Surely the important thing is ——

**Benedict** I mean, what are these tourists going to be? Young? Middle-aged? Anything. Something just to cling on to, because I'm in difficulties here.

**Estelle** (*taking a deep breath*) Well, there was some talk of a coach party of Japanese.

**Benedict** Oh God ...

**Estelle** What?

**Benedict** That just gives me huge problems. Do you know how difficult Japanese is for an actor?

**Estelle** Not really.

**Benedict** Hugely. It's hugely difficult. I mean, it's a different culture, a different value system, for a start. I mean, I just ... It would take weeks of research and reading and even after that we're probably talking several sessions with a dialect coach.

**Estelle** Sorry, I'm a bit confused. Am I giving a guided tour or are we suddenly doing a re-make of *The Seven Samurai*?

**Benedict** (*to himself, genuinely*) No, it's not something I'd feel confident with at this stage of my career.

**Estelle** Look, I'm sorry, but surely the point of ——

**Benedict** You see, at the moment I feel I have to play to my strengths, right? Wait. Listen. What about Americans? I'm comfortable with Americans. I've just done *Streetcar* in Birmingham.

**Estelle** I think there were ... I don't know. I think I remember ... let me see ... (*She shuffles through her slightly chaotic bundle of papers*) Yes! A minibus load of American war veterans and their wives.

**Benedict** War veterans! Interesting. Good. Which war? Korea? Vietnam? Vietnam would be good. OK. He's an ex-grunt, invalided out because of injury. No. Battle fatigue. Nervous exhaustion. Better.

**Estelle** Mr Thrush ...

**Benedict** (*sharply*) Sorry ... can it wait, do you think? Because when it starts to come like this — you know, the process — it really consumes all my ... He's injured as well, of course he is, in the ... So when he moves it's going to be ... (*He contorts his body to show the effect of what are obviously fairly horrific injuries*) And he's small-town America, yes. Local boy made good. A hero to the simple people of New Watford, Illinois — God! Where did that come from? I didn't know it was Illinois. Spooky, but that's the

process for you. Once you start dragging things up from inside yourself ...
And he's angry. With himself. With Vietnam. With the Army and what it's
put him through, the crippled life it's left him. Even with the girl he left
behind, who worships him ... This is fantastic! We need to do an
improvisation. You be her.

**Estelle**  Who?

**Benedict**  Mary Lou.

**Estelle**  Who? (*She looks through her sheaf of papers during the following*)

**Benedict**  The girl. The girl he left behind. The girl he no longer feels he can
face because the terrible injuries — mental and physical — that the Cong
inflicted on him in the POW camp that mean that he can't ... (*he moves his
pelvis in an erotic manner*) you know ... any more ... Let's do it — let's
impro!

**Estelle** (*looking at her papers*)  Can I ask a question?

**Benedict**  Yeah, that's good. Let's explore it. Feel free.

**Estelle**  If he's a Vietnam veteran ... why are he and his wife on a minibus tour
of East Anglia?

**Benedict**  What?

**Estelle**  Organized by the 19th US Army Air Force Field Catering Division
Veterans' Association?

**Benedict**  Ah. Point made. They're cooks. Right. Caterers. No, I couldn't do
that. Not a caterer. Nothing dramatic about catering. (*He begins a silent
catering improvisation exercise*)

**Estelle**  You obviously haven't worked for British Rail. Mr Thrush ...
Benedict! I might get on more quickly if I ...

**Benedict**  Just run through it?

**Estelle**  By myself, yes ...

**Benedict**  And I just listen and give advice?

**Estelle** (*uncertainly*)  Yes ...

**Benedict**  Just, you know, do it. For me. I'll watch. I'll listen.

**Estelle**  That's very kind of you, but really ——

**Benedict**  Listen, I've just had another really great idea.

**Estelle**  Oh.

**Benedict**  What if I sort of directed you?

**Estelle**  What?

**Benedict**  I want to direct. That's the next logical stage of my career. OK.
Right. Yep. You've got it. Whenever you're ready.

**Estelle**  Umm ... Welcome to the Theatre Royal. An historic theatre has stood
on this site since 1958, when the Mayor ——

**Benedict**  Sorry. Sorry.

**Estelle** (*snapping*)  Yes?

**Benedict**  Sorry, I'm just not clear — I mean, it's not coming off the
stage — who exactly you are.

**Estelle** What do you mean, who I am?

**Benedict** Just — who are you?

**Estelle** I told you who I am.

**Benedict** Yeah, but the problem is I just don't believe in you or what you're saying.

**Estelle** Are you calling me a liar?

**Benedict** Not exactly. Not exactly. What I'm saying is, the important thing on the stage is truth. And that outer, external truth cannot exist until the actor can find the internal truth in himself.

**Estelle** Suddenly the British Rail Catering Display Team begins to seem beautifully sane.

**Benedict** So the first question you have to ask yourself is: who am I?

*Silence*

Go on. Ask it.

**Estelle** Out loud?

**Benedict** Externalize it, yes.

**Estelle** I know who I am.

**Benedict** Do you? Do you really? I thought I knew myself, but when I looked I was just a jumble of ... a random collection of ... I don't know ... just put together with no sense of ... and a futile sort of ... you know. I was confused.

**Estelle** You don't say.

**Benedict** I'll do it. I'll show you, then you'll ... (*He takes a very deep breath and declaims in a ringing voice*) Who am I? (*Pause*) Who am I? (*Pause*) WHO AM I?

**Estelle** You are Benedict Thrush and I claim my five pounds! (*She giggles, slightly hysterically*)

**Benedict** Lie down.

**Estelle** I'm sorry?

**Benedict** On the floor.

**Estelle** This is my second best work suit!

**Benedict** On the table then.

**Estelle** No!

**Benedict** Estelle, I am only doing my best to help you realize your full inner potential. So, please — trust me.

*Estelle lies reluctantly on the operating table*

Close your eyes and breathe.

**Estelle** (*wrapping her clothes very tightly around herself*) I may have my eyes closed, but I am keeping a very close eye on you, Benedict Thrush, and at the first hint of any ...

**Benedict** Breathe. And listen to the breathing. Feel the breath going into your body. Establish a rhythm. Feel the breath. Picture it. It has a quality. A quality of light. It is light. The breath is light and it's ... you know, what's the word?

**Estelle** Shining?

**Benedict** No.

**Estelle** Gleaming?

**Benedict** No, no — penetrating. That's the word.

**Estelle** Just remember what I said, Mr Thrush.

**Benedict** It's penetrating your whole body. From head to toe. Lightness making you light. Picture it.

**Estelle** Mmm ...

**Benedict** Lifting you like a magic carpet, lifting you out of yourself, it's lifting you out of yourself ...

**Estelle** Mmmmm ... aaaah!

**Benedict** So you're floating. It's floating. It's floating above you like a shimmering magic carpet ...

**Estelle** Wheee!

**Benedict** And that's you, Estelle. That's your essence, your imagination, and it can take you anywhere. And I want it to take you back to a place where you were really, really happy. The happiest time of your life. All right?

**Estelle** Mmmmmmmm!

**Benedict** Picture it. Explore it. Feel how it felt.

**Estelle** (*obviously experiencing a highly personal, intimate moment from her past life*) Oooooh! Aaaah!

**Benedict** Good. Good.

**Estelle** Mmmmm! Whoooo!

**Benedict** (*rather alarmed at her obvious enthusiasm*) Yeah, that's fine. That's great. That's ... Now, I want you to get back on the carpet.

**Estelle** No ...

**Benedict** Do it. And it's going to take you to another place. A different place. Deep inside you. A place where you were really, really ... I mean, really, really unhappy.

**Estelle** Noooo ...

**Benedict** Yes. Do it. Go there.

**Estelle** Nnnaaaa ...

**Benedict** Picture it. Explore it. Feel it.

**Estelle** Naa, naaa, naaa ....

**Benedict** Confront it. Confront yourself.

**Estelle** Urrgh ... errgh ....

**Benedict** You can see yourself. In your imagination. It's you. You can stand outside of yourself and see yourself totally clearly.

**Estelle** Blerrgh.

**Benedict**  So describe yourself. How do you look?
**Estelle**  Fat.
**Benedict**  Good.
**Estelle**  Spotty.
**Benedict**  Excellent.
**Estelle**  Miserable.
**Benedict**  And how do you feel?
**Estelle**  Fat, spotty and miserable.
**Benedict**  Why?
**Estelle**  I've failed.
**Benedict**  How old are you?
**Estelle**  Twenty-six.
**Benedict**  (*rather disappointed*) So this is ... Oh. You don't want to go back to early childhood? Only, I'm better with early childhood —
**Estelle**  (*suddenly crying out*)  Derek!
**Benedict**  (*startled*)  Derek?
**Estelle**  The Divisional Manager, Catering. He said he'd leave his wife. He was lovely, in a sort of slightly more mature ... I resolved that I was never going to, not with a married man, but as soon as I smelt his hair gel I knew. And God knows I was at all-time low after Kevin ...
**Benedict**  Kevin?
**Estelle**  My fiancé. Ex-fiancé. He'd just broken it off. I was in such a vulnerable ... So when Derek's hand accidentally brushed my bottom as we were reviewing the portion control figures, I knew that I was going to, that it was inevitable ... I gave him everything. Everything! Things that I'd never given anyone before, not even Kevin, in the entire seven years of our engagement. And then for Derek to come to me and say that he couldn't go on with the guilt of betraying his wife and children and, oh, by the way, I was redundant ... So that's where I am. On that day. That day that Derek walked into my office with his lovely crinkly hair and big hands and said ... and said ... I can see myself. Fat. Spotty ...
**Benedict**  Miserable.
**Estelle**  Miserable, yes. I'm a failure! A total and utter failure! (*She heaves about with racking sobs and sighs*)
**Benedict**  Good. Good. Yes! Confront that failure! Face up to that truth about yourself and use it! Good! So now just get back on the magic carpet. Bring yourself back. You're still breathing. Aren't you? And you're coming back, coming back, coming back — and you're back. Good. Good. That was — interesting. Really interesting. So — how do you feel?

*Estelle wails*

Yeah, it can make you feel a bit — you know — funny. Because you're doing something that ordinary people never normally do at all. Facing the truth, the real truth about yourself. But that's something that an actor has to do every day. We have to. It's what acting's all about. Caring. Listening. Responding.

*There is a pause. Estelle sobs hopelessly*

Anyway, I think you'll find that'll help you with your — little talk when you come to do it. Oh, hey, look is that the time? I've got to dash. It's crucial that I see someone before they ... otherwise there's going to be ... I'll catch you later. Glad to be of ... you know.

*Benedict exits and instantly re-enters*

Break a leg.

*He exits*

*After whimpering for a moment, Estelle gets off the table, dabbing her eyes. She takes up a position at the front of the stage, scrabbles through her notes, sniffs loudly. She pulls out a distinctively coloured piece of paper and, unseeing, blows her nose on it. She stuffs the paper into a pocket, takes a deep breath and begins her speech*

**Estelle**  Ladies and Gentlemen, welcome to ... welcome to ... the ... Theatre Royal ... (*But her voice gets fainter and fainter and she dissolves into tears*)

*The Lights change*

*The usherettes appear. They gather around Estelle*

**Jacintha**  Poor love.
**Petronella**  Poor lamb.
**Petronella** } (*together*) Poor heart.
**Jacintha** }
**Wendy** (*holding out a handkerchief*) Blow.

*Estelle takes the handkerchief and blows her nose. She gradually cheers up during the following*

**Jacintha**  She came to the theatre hoping for escape.
**Petronella**  A mistake.
**Jacintha**  Theatre makes us face up to what we are.

**Petronella**  Makes us confront ourselves.
**Jacintha**  Which wounds.
**Petronella**  Which shocks.
**Jacintha**  And makes us question what we are.

*During the following, Petronella and Jacintha gyrate dramatically as they speak. Wendy joins in, reluctantly*

**Petronella** ⎫
**Jacintha** ⎭ (*together*) Round and round ——
**Petronella** — the question goes inside the skull.
**Petronella** ⎫
**Jacintha** ⎭ (*together*) Round and round ——
**Jacintha** — to be or not to be?
**Petronella** ⎫
**Jacintha** ⎭ (*together*) Round and round ——
**Jacintha** — tomorrow and tomorrow and tomorrow ——
**Petronella** ⎫
**Jacintha** ⎭ (*together*) Round and round ——
**Wendy**  I've got a bit of a headache.
**Jacintha**  But after the suffering comes — the healing.
**Petronella**  The benison.
**Jacintha**  The wisdom.
**Petronella** ⎫
**Jacintha** ⎬ (*together*)  Pain. Catharsis. Wholeness. Tranquillity. The magic
**Wendy** ⎭                            of theatre.

*Estelle, more cheerful now, gives her nose a final blow*

**Estelle**  Right. Be brave, Estelle. The day can only get better.

*Estelle strides purposefully off*

**Petronella** ⎫
**Jacintha** ⎬ (*together*)  Bless. Love.
**Wendy** ⎭
**Petronella**  But who comes here?

*Zara Roscoff enters. She is a glamorous figure in a slightly overblown way, a real actress, dressed extravagantly in an expensive outdoor coat which she wraps around herself. She has a handbag and a copy of the "Daily Telegraph"*

**Petronella** ⎫
**Jacintha** ⎭ (*together*) Our star!

**Wendy** Oh good. A bit of glamour at last.

*The usherettes form a ceremonial archway with their torches, down which Zara parades*

**Petronella** ⎫
**Jacintha** ⎬ (*together*) Miss Zara Roscoff.
**Wendy** ⎭
**Petronella** Star of stage and screen.
**Wendy** The small screen. A sitcom well past its best.
**Jacintha** And many, many stage appearances too numerous to mention.
**Petronella** In some of our most cherished centres of theatrical excellence.
**Wendy** Stevenage. Dartford. Harlow. Swindon.

*Zara's husband Hugo enters and walks down the avenue of torches. He is dressed like a rather stuffy bank manager, with a briefcase*

**Petronella** ⎫ (*together*) And her husband! Henry!
**Jacintha** ⎭
**Wendy** Hugo!
**Petronella** ⎫ (*together*) Hugo!
**Jacintha** ⎭

*Zara and Hugo stand frozen in an artificial embrace. They are all smiles. There might even be the flashing of a few cameras*

**Petronella** Who is ...
**Jacintha** Who is ...

*They seem at a loss to say anything about Hugo. Petronella and Jacintha produce Fecund programmes and study them*

**Petronella** Ah, here we are! "One of the theatre's most selfless actors."
**Wendy** He never gets big parts.
**Jacintha** "He has developed a wide range of interests outside of the theatre."
**Wendy** He hasn't had a part since 1985.
**Petronella** "Extensive work on radio, which he loves."
**Wendy** He doesn't have to learn the lines.

*The next caption appears. It reads "10.05 hours. Happy Returns"*

**Petronella** ⎫
**Jacintha** ⎬ (*together*) "10.05 hours. Happy Returns."
**Wendy** ⎭

*Hugo and Zara stand frozen, smiling*

*The usherettes exit*

**Hugo** Can I stop smiling now?
**Zara** (*unfreezing*) You can do what you like.

*They both lose their cheesey smiles instantly and look irritated and impatient*

**Hugo** My jaws ache.
**Zara** Try smiling more often. Once a decade would do wonders. You'd be
surprised.

*Hugo sits at the operating table with a sigh and settles down to work with a
calculator, making the odd note on a sheet of paper. Zara, still wrapped in
her outdoor coat, puts on a pair of fashionable glasses and sits down to do
the* Telegraph *crossword*

**Hugo** The local press. God, journalists. So bloody tedious.
**Zara** One press conference in seven years and he's suffering from over-
exposure.
**Hugo** She was their forestry and aboriculture correspondent, did you know
that? The one with the glasses and speech impediment.
**Zara** That wasn't a speech impediment, it was a regional accent. Which
you'd know if you bothered to tour more often.
**Hugo** (*in a yokel's accent*) "I just do the theatre on the side. I normally writes
about wood."
**Zara** You're guaranteed a good notice, then, darling.
**Hugo** I don't know how you do this, week after week. Crappy plays, terrible
hotels. Godforsaken holes like this. God, the provinces.
**Zara** It's a marvellous play.

*Hugo snorts*

You never could judge a script.
**Hugo** I bow to your superior judgement, darling.
**Zara** The way Roland gets inside my woman's mind. For a man to do that,
it's uncanny. How does Roland know how it feels to be inside a woman?
**Hugo** Lots of practice, if the rumours are true.
**Zara** He knows how it feels to be just a piece of sexual machinery, only there
to give a man pleasure, totally dependant on his will, his power. How does
he know that? How does he know how that feels?
**Hugo** He must have read it in *Cosmopolitan*.

**Zara** Oh, piss off, Hugo ...

**Hugo** It's what passes for research with writers like Roland. Anyway, how do you know?

**Zara** How do I know what?

**Hugo** How it feels to be a sexual machine.

**Zara** I'm an actress.

**Hugo** Aha.

**Zara** It's certainly not from my experience of the marital bed ...

**Hugo** Oh Christ, Zara. Not my shortcomings in the bedroom department monologue again.

**Zara** Interesting you chose that word, darling.

**Hugo** What word?

**Zara** Shortcomings.

**Hugo** Get stuffed.

*There is a pause. Hugo works*

**Zara** Are you going over your lines?

**Hugo** No.

**Zara** Well, you should be. Because you nearly went last night. I could see it in your eyes. You looked like a village idiot on mogadon. Just don't dry this afternoon, and leave me with an egg.

*Hugo works on*

Oh, will you stop shuffling those pieces of paper around! If you're not studying, what are doing?

**Hugo** Your quarterly VAT returns.

**Zara** God. You really have become dreary, haven't you? You're an actor, Hugo. Allegedly. Not a certified accountant!

**Hugo** As you never tire of pointing out, darling, normally when I'm trying to get to sleep, you're the one who earns the money in this partnership. I'm the one who looks after it and makes sure the tax gets paid. And if I don't finish these today, we'll get fined an excess, so if you'll excuse me ...

**Zara** Bastard. Now you've made me get hot and we've got another photocall in five minutes! (*She takes off her coat to reveal a hospital gown absolutely covered in blood and revolting-looking stains*)

**Hugo** (*looking up and taking in the dress*) Not another Vivienne Westwood?

**Zara** This is my costume, Hugo. For the photocall. As you are very well aware.

**Hugo** I could have sworn it was that thing you wore for the BAFTAs.

**Zara** Which side of the bed did you get out of this morning?

**Hugo** Yours.

*There is a pause*

**Zara**  I couldn't sleep. I went for a walk.

**Hugo**  Of course. And you took your spongebag for company.

**Zara**  I took a shower. And since we're checking up, I might ask you where you were all yesterday afternoon.

**Hugo** Cricket match.

**Zara**  In a godforsaken hole like this?

**Hugo**  Minor County.

*There is a pause. Pleased, Hugo works. He reaches across to Zara's handbag and pulls out an untidy wodge of receipts*

Zara, how many times have I told you to keep your receipts ...

**Zara**  (*noticing and moving quickly towards him*) What are you doing? How dare you look in my ... don't!

*But it is too late. A condom has come out of the bag with the receipts. Hugo picks it up and examines it critically. Zara walks away*

**Hugo**  What is this? (*He waves the condom around*)

**Zara**  (*not entirely convincingly*)  What's that, darling?

**Hugo**  This? This is ... (*he reads the label*) a *Red Hot Raunchy Rubber Tickler*. (*He looks more closely*) Acacia Honey Flavour. That's what this is.

**Zara**  Is it? And what are you going to do with it?

**Hugo**  I'm going to ask it what it was doing in your handbag.

**Zara**  Yes, that's about your limit with condoms, isn't it?

**Hugo**  Zara ...

**Zara**  It was ... It was ... just in case.

**Hugo**  Just in case? Just in case? Just in case WHAT?

**Zara**  Just in case a miracle happened and you had a spontaneous rush of blood to the head.

**Hugo**  The head?

**Zara**  Wherever — don't be pedantic.

**Hugo**  I think that is extremely unlikely, don't you?

**Zara**  Extremely, yes, since you ask.

**Hugo**  And even if — God forbid — I succumbed to a testosterone-induced coma of passion for you and your increasingly saggy physical charms, this thing would be about as much use to me as a ham sandwich at a bar mitzvah, wouldn't it?

**Zara**  What are you going on about, Hugo?

**Hugo**  The vasectomy is what I'm going on about.

**Zara**  What vasectomy?

**Hugo** My vasectomy!

*There is a pause*

**Zara** Oh.
**Hugo** Ten years ago. The unkindest cut of all. My little sacrifice to our career.

*There is a pause*

**Zara** Fuck. I forgot.
**Hugo** You forgot.
**Zara** I can't remember everything.
**Hugo** If you'd been anything like a proper wife ——
**Zara** A proper wife! What do you mean, a proper wife?
**Hugo** The scar might have reminded you.
**Zara** I wasn't looking for a scar.
**Hugo** You weren't looking full stop. My adam's apple's the furthest south
you've been in years.
**Zara** How dare you say I haven't been a proper wife!
**Hugo** You haven't.
**Zara** Well, what have I been?
**Hugo** A bloody actress, that's what. A self-obsessed, inward-looking,
"nobody else in the world matters a toss" bloody — actress! That's what
I mean. My career this! My career that! This part, that part, this audition,
that audition. "They didn't want me, Hugo. I feel rejected." "My public.
My audience." Day after day. Night after night. Year after year! That's
what I bloody well mean! (*Pause*) So who was it, darling? Or do I mean
is it?
**Zara** Nobody you'd know. Nobody. Oh, I don't know ... Everybody.
**Hugo** *Everybody*?
**Zara** It's been so long since you've had any work you've forgotten what it's
like to be on tour. You can't imagine what it's like to be stuck in somewhere
like, oh, I don't know, Billingham during the day. I mean, what do you do
in Billingham during the day?
**Hugo** Most of the cast, by the sound of it.
**Zara** Don't get sanctimonious with me, Hugo. I wouldn't have had to — if
you condescended to come on tour with me, as I wanted. I wanted you with
me but you weren't there, so are you surprised I turned to others? I have
relied upon the kindness of strangers.
**Hugo** Spare me the Blanche bloody Dubois.
**Zara** I was a bloody good Blanche Dubois.
**Hugo** You were a terrible Blanche Dubois. Others? My God, you make it
sound like the entire male membership of Equity. How many have there
been?

*Zara shrugs insouciantly*

Let's have a roll call, then.

**Zara** Oh, really, Hugo ...

**Hugo** (*moving to the table and rifling through the VAT receipts*) Let's have a look at the VAT invoices and see who's had the pleasure of horizontal duologues with you in the last three months. Let's see. *All My Sons* in Gateshead. *All* your sons, was it? Isn't that incest? To say nothing of crowded?

**Zara** Funny man.

**Hugo** *The Trojan Women* in Matlock. Well, not too many possibilities there.

**Zara** You think so?

**Hugo** What? (*Realization dawns*) My God ...

**Zara** Needs must in Matlock.

**Hugo** (*slightly thrown by this*) *Goldilocks and the Three Bears* at Harrogate. Obviously not so much a case of "Who's been sleeping in my bed?" as "Who hasn't?" Then there was *'Tis Pity She's A Whore* ...

**Zara** Yes, all right, all right. Don't go on.

**Hugo** All right. Fair enough. What's done is done and cannot be undone ... nnnargh!

**Zara** ⎫
          ⎬ (*together*) Scottish play!
**Hugo** ⎭

*They cross their fingers, twirl round three times and do the silly things that actors do when the dreaded play is quoted*

**Hugo** What I meant was — all that's water under the bridge ——
**Zara** Don't you mean spermicide under the diaphragm?
**Hugo** — but what I do want to know is — who was it last night?

*Zara is silent*

Tell me, Zara. I want to know who you were with last night. Tell me or I'll ...

**Zara** You'll what? What will you do? You can't live without my money, you can't move out of the house because you've got nowhere else to go, and you're not even going to hit me because you think you're such a restrained so-bloody-English gentleman. Which you're not, by the way, because as far as I remember you never did take the weight on your elbows. So what are you going to do, Hugo, darling? What exactly are you going to do?

**Hugo** Smile.

**Zara** What?

**Hugo** Smile.

*There is a sudden burst of flashguns*

    *The usherettes return. Wendy has a small flash camera and kneels to take*
    *a photograph*

*Slowly, ghastly smiles appear on Hugo and Zara's faces. They go back into*
*their stiff artificial freeze*

**Petronella**⎫
**Jacintha**  ⎬ (*together*) Smile!
**Wendy**   ⎭

*Zara and Hugo smile for the camera, posed in a spontaneous posture*

**Petronella** Aaaah! Look at their faces!
**Jacintha** A pose for their public.
**Petronella** Who love them to bits.
**Wendy** A showbiz marriage.
**Petronella** Made in heaven. Off they go ——
**Jacintha**   ⎫ (*together*) To the bliss of ——
**Petronella** ⎭
**Jacintha** — the marital dressing room.
**Petronella**⎫
**Jacintha**  ⎬ (*together*) Love. Bless.
**Wendy**   ⎭

    *Zara and Hugo exit, their faces fixed in an unconvincing grimace of*
    *marital harmony*

    *Roland enters and freezes. He is a rather shabby dissolute figure who looks*
    *as though he has seen better times*

**Jacintha** And who is this?
**Wendy** They know who it is. It's just posturing.
**Petronella** Luckett.
**Wendy** Pardon?
**Petronella** Luckett.
**Jacintha** Roland.
**Petronella**⎫
**Jacintha**  ⎬ (*together*) The author!
**Wendy**   ⎭
**Petronella** Of "Fecund".
**Jacintha** He's overflowing with the dramatic muse.

*Roland heads for the exit and collides with a wing flat*

   *He exits*

**Wendy**  He's full to the gills with lunchtime booze.
**Petronella**  He's been set for exams.
**Wendy**  Once.
**Petronella**       By teachers across the land he's rated.
**Wendy**            And by thousands of students totally hated.
**Jacintha**         Because he's a writer we're speaking in verse.
**Wendy**            I think we should go before things get worse.

*Wendy changes the slide/caption: "14.05 hours. Doing You."*

**All**  14.05 hours. *Doing You.*

*Roland enters and stands C, looking out at the auditorium. He has probably
had a good lunch, especially in the liquid department. He stands. He
breathes deeply. He gestures expansively*

**Roland**  The Empty Space. (*He smiles, ruefully*) Poor, dear, misguided little
Peter Brook. (*He smiles, forgivingly*)

*Estelle enters from the wings. She is obviously in a hurry to be elsewhere.
Seeing Roland she grimaces slightly, puts her head down and makes for the
other wing*

   It's Estelle, isn't it?
**Estelle**  It is, yes.
**Roland**  We met before. At lunchtime, if you remember?
**Estelle**  I remember.
**Roland**  I hope you can find it in your heart to forgive me, Estelle.
**Estelle**  What for?
**Roland**  For the unfortunate incident in the cafeteria queue, when I was
   thrown against you with my jumbo sausage ...
**Estelle**  Forget it. Really.
**Roland**  So as far as you are concerned the incident is closed?
**Estelle**  So far as I'm concerned there never was an incident.

*Roland absorbs this and is not unhappy to make another start*

**Roland**  I am a playwright, Estelle.
**Estelle**  I know.

**Roland** My name is ——

**Estelle** Roland Luckett. Born 1945, educated at Merchant Bankers' School, Uffington and St Mungo's College, Cambridge. Married five times. Works include ——

**Roland** You know me better than I know myself! Excellent! But I should have expected this. Obviously this is part of your brief as Marketing Manager. The first rule of marketing: know your product.

**Estelle** The second rule, in point of fact, but actually, no — we did you at school.

**Roland** Did me?

**Estelle** As a, you know — set text. Are you all right?

**Roland** I'm just trying to imagine being "done" by a whole generation of schoolgirls. I'm sorry. I'm back with you. Presumably this was for your A levels.

**Estelle** GCSE.

**Roland** (*disappointed*) Oh ... oh well. Just as a matter of interest — indulge me for a moment — was this an all-girls' school?

**Estelle** Worst luck.

**Roland** Did it have a uniform?

**Estelle** Oh yes.

**Roland** Did it? Did it? Gymslips compulsory, were they?

**Estelle** I'm sorry?

**Roland** Nothing. Tell me, which play of mine did you study?

**Estelle** Oh Lord, now you're asking. I enjoyed it, though. I think. I seemed to be in stitches all the time, anyway.

**Roland** Excellent! Music to the ears of a creative artist, believe me. But surely you can remember what play it was? Surely it can't have been that long ago. A young attractive gymslipped thing like yourself ...

**Estelle** It had ... well, there was a man and a woman ——

**Roland** Yes.

**Estelle** — and then another man and another woman came in ——

**Roland** What we call plot development, yes.

**Estelle** — then some more people came in and talked and talked and talked; then some of the people who came in at first went out, but then some new people came in, and one of the women who came in earlier, went out but came back in again and said something really, really important — I can't remember what — to one of the men who I always imagined as having a ginger moustache. And then they kissed a lot and had a glass of ice-cold champagne and that was more or less it.

**Roland** I can't quite place that one.

**Estelle** It had a brown cover.

**Roland** Tell me, Estelle, do you find it aphrodisiac? Meeting a well-known creative person. Because I've found that many women ——

**Estelle** (*lost in her recollections*) It's funny how you remember things, isn't it? "We'll have a glass of ice-cold champagne, darling". I remember that vividly, but I can't even remember the story. Funny, isn't it?

**Roland** Do you like ice-cold champagne, Estelle? Because I have a very comfortable room in a nearby local hotel, and in the little fridge there just happens to be ——

**Estelle** And now I come to think of it, it was another man who had the little ginger moustache.

**Roland** Can we leave the ginger moustache to one side for a moment, Estelle? What I'm saying is that I think I may go and have a post-prandial glass of champagne and a little lie down. Perhaps you'd care to join me?

*Estelle laughs to herself*

What?

**Estelle** Nothing.

**Roland** What are you laughing at? Ah! You're remembering my play. An amusing moment, a witty riposte. Is it turning you on?

**Estelle** What? No. I've just remembered what the teacher said. (*She laughs more and more hysterically during the following*)

**Roland** Teacher? What teacher?

**Estelle** The one who taught us your book for GCSE.

**Roland** And?

*Estelle continues to laugh hysterically*

What? Please!

**Estelle** No, I can't ... I couldn't possibly ...

**Roland** Estelle, I want to know what was said. It was obviously ... very funny. I want to share the joke.

**Estelle** (*trying to be serious*) Oh. It's not a joke. (*She bursts out laughing again*) The teacher said — I don't know how to put this — she said that it was quite obvious that the person who wrote the play was obviously absolutely terrified of women and wasn't secure in his own sexuality.

**Roland** She said that?

**Estelle** And that's you, isn't it? (*She screams with laughter*)

**Roland** That's very funny.

**Estelle** Yes, that's why I was ——

**Roland** What made her say that?

**Estelle** I don't know, as I said ...

**Roland** Who was she, this woman? Do I know her?

**Estelle** She was — I don't know — I can't remember her ...

**Roland** Was this a convent school? Was she a nun? It must have been, given your description: young girls in uniforms, gymslips ——

**Estelle** I never said ——
**Roland** So — some old repressed, frigid nun who has never even set eyes
on me presumes to question, to make assumptions, to make *jokes*, for
God's sake, about my sexuality to a class of tittering, gymslipped
adolescent girls, simply because my writing dares to challenge conven-
tional notions of morality and religion ——
**Estelle** Miss Thruxton!
**Roland** What?
**Estelle** I've remembered. Our English teacher. Miss Thruxton.
**Roland** Not a nun, then? Miss Thruxton. Well, the name says it all, doesn't
it? A dried-out, shrivelled up old spinster, I'll be bound? With a bicycle.
Oh, no, I'm with you. I've got her. Feminist type. Porcupine hair, nasal
whine, dungarees and boots. Rolled her own.
**Estelle** About twenty-five. Long dark curls. Fabulous figure. Drove a little
sports car. Non-smoker. We all had crushes on her in the second year.
**Roland** I see. And what was the basis of her devastating insight into the depth
of my sexual nature?
**Estelle** She said that the titles of your plays were very revealing. Tell me
some titles.
**Roland** I — can't seem to remember them just at the moment.
**Estelle** "A Finger In The Dyke". That's one, isn't it?
**Roland** Yes, but ... the meaning of the word — has changed since ——
**Estelle** "Bitchkill". That's another one. You see? Shows that you hate
women, that you want to kill them.
**Roland** Rubbish! The title was a pure fluke! It came to me in a flash ...
**Estelle** While you were having a blazing row with your third wife.
**Roland** How do you know that?
**Estelle** Miss Thruxton ——
**Roland** How I'm growing to loathe that name.
**Estelle** — saw you on a chat show.
**Roland** Did she? Did she?
**Estelle** And then there's "Fecund". I wonder what Miss Thruxton would
make of that? I'd guess that her line on it would be that you have this terrible
fear of the mess of sex and babies and so on. That you're afraid of women's
sexual appetites and the sexual act itself. Something like that. Well, I've
enjoyed our little chat, but I must be getting on. I'll try and think what that
title was.
**Roland** Please — don't bother.
**Estelle** Bye.

*Estelle exits*

*A few seconds later Mo enters*

**Mo** You'll have to shift, Roland. I'm opening the house for the matinée. You all right?

**Roland** I've been better.

**Mo** (*sitting next to Roland*) Drawn another blank? Look on the bright side. What would you have found to talk about afterwards?

**Roland** Who cares about afterwards? (*He brightens slightly*) You're right, though. The young ones always go post-coitally flakey. Much my favourite kind of woman is one who has lived, and learned from experience. Who wishes to share with a kindred spirit. Who can operate on an intellectual, as well as a physical level. Someone who understands the needs of the soul as well as the needs of the flesh. I do have a very comfortable room in a nearby local hotel ... (*He puts his hand on Mo's knee*)

*Mo looks down and considers the hand, then deliberately removes it from her knee*

**Mo** You've forgotten about last night, then?

**Roland** Last night?

**Mo** On this very table. You have forgotten. But don't worry. There wasn't much to remember, in point of fact.

**Roland** (*the light dawning horribly*) What?

**Mo** Forget it. I have. It doesn't matter. It could happen to any bloke. Especially after the amount you'd had to drink.

**Roland** (*lowering his head into his hands*) Oh God ...

**Mo** Only do us a favour and don't mention it to Deirdre, will you?

**Roland** Deirdre?

**Mo** My other half. She's very possessive. She's also a blue belt in kendo. And now I'm opening the house. The stage is live.

*Mo exits*

**Roland** (*looking around him, stunned*) Lucky old stage.

*The Lights fade to blackout*

*Roland exits*

*The Lights come up on a different setting*

*The usherettes enter*

**All** Clear the stage!

**Petronella** Standby lights!

**Jacintha** Standby sound!
**Petronella** Standby front of house!
**Wendy** Is that us?
**All** And we're off!
**Jacintha** The matinée.

*The actors enter at high speed. Hugo is there, of course, plus the others —
including Benedict — in operating theatre gowns and face masks*

*The idea is that the cast rattle through "Fecund" at high speed, underpinning
the usherettes' dialogue. During the following they arrange implements and
have (unheard) dialogue with each other*

*The usherettes take their seats at the side of the stage and watch*

**Jacintha** Good house?
**Petronella** About two thirds.
**Wendy** Empty.

*Zara enters, heavily pregnant, in a wheelchair*

*The usherettes applaud Zara's entry. Zara gets up rapidly from her wheelchair
and makes an impassioned (but unheard) speech at the front of the stage.
Then she gets back on to the operating table*

**Jacintha** She's marvellous.
**Petronella** Wonderful.
**Jacintha** Such a pro.

*Zara gets off the table again and has an impassioned dialogue with Benedict
at the front of the stage*

**Petronella** He's good.
**Jacintha** He's very good. There's such an electricity ——
**Petronella** A real chemistry ...
**Petronella** } (*together*) — between them both.
**Jacintha** }
**Jacintha** Magic. Pure magic. It's what theatre's all about. Bliss.

*Zara gets back on to the table and Benedict retreats upstage. Hugo comes to
the front and makes a silent speech. Even though we can't hear him, he seems
rather hesitant and unsure of himself*

**Petronella** Oh, look. It's Henry.

**Wendy**  Hugo.
**Petronella**⎫
**Jacintha**⎬ (*together*) Hugo.

*They watch for a moment. There seems to be nothing else to say. During the
following, things seem come to some sort of climax on the stage*

**Petronella**⎫
**Jacintha**⎬ (*together*) Love. Bless.

   *All the actors, except Hugo and Zara, leave*

*Hugo and Zara have a big moment — or rather Zara does — and they both
freeze in a dramatic posture. There is a lighting change to indicate that the
curtain has come down. A faint, polite ripple of applause from beyond the
curtain*

   *Zara remonstrates briefly with Hugo, then sweeps off the stage. Hugo
   plods off after her*

**Petronella**⎫
**Jacintha**⎬(*together*)  Interval!
**Wendy**  That was quick.
**Jacintha**  Our busiest time.
**Petronella**  Ice-creams.
**Jacintha**  Programmes.
**Wendy**  Toilets.
**Petronella**⎫
**Jacintha**⎬ (*together*) Our public. Excuse us.

   *The usherettes exit*

*The stage is left empty for a moment. We hear the murmur of an elderly
audience moaning about the price of everything*

   *Petronella and Jacintha return*

**Petronella**  God, I am *exhausted*!
**Jacintha** (*to Petronella*) Darling, you were marvellous.
**Petronella**  Was I? I didn't think I ——
**Jacintha**  Out of this world! I've never seen you do anything better. Fab, fab,
   *fab!*

*There is a pause. They seem to have run out of compliments*

**Petronella** Where's Wendy?

*They look around and shrug, then sit on their seats*

**Petronella**⎱ (*together*) Second half.
**Jacintha** ⎰

*The actors—including Benedict, Zara and Hugo—resume their positions ready for the second half of "Fecund". Benedict and Zara are* DS

*The Lights change as if the curtain is going up and they are off on the second half. Benedict and Zara are playing a poignant farewell scene*

**Petronella** This is a lovely bit.
**Jacintha** Moving.
**Petronella** Poignant.
**Jacintha** I think I'm going to cry.
**Petronella** Mind your mascara.

*Wendy appears, making her way noisily to her seat. During the following, the actors arrange themselves as follows: Zara on the operating table, with the group of medics, including Hugo and Benedict, in full operating gear, grouped around her, all acting away like mad at delivering a baby*

**Wendy** Sorry. Sorry. I got locked in.

*The others glare at her*

Have I missed much?
**Petronella**⎱ (*together*) It's nearly the end.
**Jacintha** ⎰
**Wendy** Is it. (*Under her breath*) Thank God for that.

*The lighting changes on stage and the pace of the performance slows to something approaching normal speed*

*Wendy changes the slide/caption to: "16.30 hours. Dry."*

*There is a huge scream from Zara and we are into the real time matinée performance of "Fecund", somewhere very near the end of the piece. Zara is acting her heart out. There is the regular beep of a heart monitoring machine. There is also the odd cough and rustle of a sweet paper from what is obviously quite a small, elderly and not very engaged audience*

**Hugo** Push! Push! You must push! Summon all your strength to push out the life, the new life!

**Zara** Push, he says, the one with the cruel eyes and the cold scientist's hands. I am pushing! Oh! The pain! So much pain ... I didn't know there was so much pain in the world ... Aah! Ah! Ah! Aaaah!

**Hugo** (*turning to the audience*) It's all about blood in the end. Blood and mess and pain and guilt.

**Zara** The woman bearing the man's load of guilt.

**Hugo** He has no part of it now. The man. The miracle is no longer his. He is apart. His job is done. He is half of the double helix. A cipher in the genetic code. That is his immortality.

**Zara** And I am their victim. But his victim most of all. Him. Who did this to me. Who pushed something in me, and left a part of himself, only so that I may push out his legacy nine agonizing months later. And they say I should be grateful? Have I given my permission? Do I consent? No! Ah! Aaah!

**Hugo** Push, now! Push! That the miracle may at last be accomplished! Push! Push! Push! One more push and nature's triumph is complete. It's ... (*He stiffens and freezes momentarily*)

*Something very strange happens to the quality of the light. The heart monitor beep gradually slows down and stops. All the actors on the stage begin to move in extreme slow motion and only Hugo moves and speaks at the normal rate. His movements and facial expressions, though, suggest that the words that he speaks are what is racing through his head. The others show no sign of hearing him. We share Hugo's perceptions and nobody else's. He turns to face the audience*

Oh fuck. I've dried. Shit. Shit, shit, shit. What is it? What is it? Think. Think! Bloody hell. And we're only a few moments from the end of the sodding thing. A few seconds away from a shower and a stiff gin. I can almost taste it. (*He pauses*) Funny what happens to time when you dry. It feels like hours passing but you know it can only be microseconds. Or perhaps I've passed out and it is hours. Can't tell. The brains turn to loft insulation and everything else slows down. Except the bowels, which turn to liquid fertiliser. No good. I'll just have to wait for the prompt. (*He pauses. Perhaps he shuffles a little to one side*) Yes, come on, come on, dear. Where is she? It must be deafeningly obvious I've dried by now. Oh God, perhaps she thinks it's a pause? Or a silence, as Roland calls them. What is the difference between a pause and a silence? I read a definition once. By Harold Pinter. No. Forgotten it. (*He looks at Zara*) Look at her glaring at me. It's no good looking at me like that, you stupid cow! I can't remember. We're just going to have to wait for the prompt to get back from her holidays. God, she looks pissed off. So it's not all bad.

*There is a slightly exaggerated shuffling sound from the auditorium*

Hallo. Fifteenth row's getting restless. They can tell something's gone wrong. I can hear them sucking their dentures. Why does an audience cluster at the back, even when the theatre's empty? Perhaps it's the spit from the stage? Come to that, why *do* actors spit when they speak on the stage? I mean, you don't spit when you talk in real life, but you get up here and suddenly, whoosh! It's the Trevi Fountain. I could write one of those coffee table books about it: "Great Theatrical Gobbers Of Our Time". (*He pauses*) And so we pass into the dying years of the twentieth century and still no sign of a prompt. I wish I was at home with a herbal tea and the *Financial Times*. Ah. Here we go. Here it comes. The Kraken wakes.

*A strange, blurred and slowed-down voice echoes muddily through the ether. It is recognizably a female voice, it may even be recognizably Mo's voice, but what it says is totally indistinct and unrecognizable, at least to Hugo's ears*

What the hell was that supposed to be? Couldn't make out a bloody word. (*He staggers slightly*) I've got a sort of rushing in my ears and I feel light-headed. Perhaps I'm going to have a heart attack! That'd teach her. Making me do this. Pretending to be someone else. Bloody childish way to earn a living. (*He looks around*) Quite pleasant up here when you get the chance to have a look around. (*His face suddenly turns vicious*) Who was it? Who was it? I have to find out. Who was she with last night?

*Benedict looks at Hugo*

(*Accidentally catching Benedict's eye*) Look at him. He's enjoying this. My discomfiture. Arrogant young bastard. Eyes like pissholes in the snow, but a mouth like a ... Hold on. Hold hard. Of course! He's in that bloody sitcom with her! She wasn't in bed when I woke up this morning because she was at his digs with him! Yes. All those whispered conversations in the corner of the dressing room. She keeps giving him her brave little smile. It all fits together! They had the opportunity, they had the means and they had the motive. I've been in too many Agatha Christies. It's him! It must be him! It's been going on right under my nose! Treacherous little bastard! And all those promises he made to me yesterday afternoon! Bloody hell! Yes? Prompt!

*The blurred voice is heard again, but this time it is not so blurred. During the following the lights gradually return to normal and the other actors come up to normal speed*

What's that? Speak up, Maureen! For pity's sake, speak up!

*And Mo's totally normal voice gives the prompt. Even so, all we hear is a voice from the wings. Hugo hears it, though, and strides up to Zara on the table. Lots of shouting. Zara screams a lot. Hugo fiddles none too gently with Zara under the blankets and pulls out a very bloody, very messy baby doll. Zara screams even more. Hugo holds the baby aloft like a trophy*

It's ... a girl!
**Mo** (*off stage*) It's a boy.
**Hugo** It's a boy!

*The Lights fade to give the impression of a front curtain coming down. The actors line up rapidly to form a curtain call. There is a good deal of hissing and spitting between Hugo and Zara and a lot of malevolent glaring from Hugo to Benedict*

*The Lights change to indicate the curtain going up. There is unenthusiastic applause. The company takes a bow. Benedict steps forward to take an individual bow. As he turns back, Hugo bops him on the nose. Benedict doubles over, his hands to his nose, trying to stem the bleeding. Hugo and Zara step forward to take a bow together, then rejoin the company line for a final company bow*

*The Lights change to indicate the curtain coming down. As soon as it has, Zara turns sharply to Hugo and knees him viciously in the groin. He doubles over with pain*

*Zara walks off without looking back*

*The two men glare at each other through their respective pain and stagger off*

*The Lights change to a semi-lit state. The usherettes move on to the stage*

*Under the following the stage is changed from the stage to the auditorium of the theatre by the backstage crew and other members of the cast. The main aisle is* c; *with a doorway from a staircase* us. *There are doors to the Gents' and Ladies' lavatories* us. *There is rubbish in the aisles; what we see reinforces everything that we have heard about the tattiness of the place so far*

*The usherettes either make a performance of helping or they take forever moving inessential items, faff about and generally get in the way*

**Petronella** The play moves on.
**Jacintha** The drama never ends.
**Petronella** On the stage.
**Jacintha** In the wings.
**Petronella** Behind the stage.
**Jacintha** In the dressing rooms.
**Wendy** The least said about that, the better.
**Jacintha** But what you see is just the tip.
**Petronella** We're the ones up here.
**Jacintha** The lucky ones, trapped in the remorseless, unpitying glare of the spotlights ——
**Petronella** — like rabbits caught in the headlamps.
**Jacintha** Transfixed.
**Petronella** Hypnotized.
**Wendy** Full of ourselves.
**Jacintha** But there are others ...
**Petronella** The ones back there, lurking in their little places in the darkness ...
**Jacintha** The ones you never see.
**Petronella** Until today.
**Jacintha** Underpaid.
**Petronella** Undervalued.
**Wendy** Under-endowed.

*Petronella and Jacintha look at Wendy*

Intellectually, I meant.
**Jacintha** The crew.
**Petronella** The techies.
**Jacintha** SMs.
**Petronella** ASMs.
**Jacintha** DSMs.
**Wendy** MBEs, CBEs, DFCs and bar.
**Petronella** Lighting wizards.
**Jacintha** Sound magicians.
**Petronella** Cossy conjurors.
**Wendy** People who hump scenery.
**Petronella** They have a language all their own.
**Jacintha** LX.
**Petronella** QX.
**Jacintha** SFX.
**Wendy** *In nomine, domine deus ex machina techiensis. Amen.*

**All** The backstage, backroom boys and girls, without whom none of this, et
  cetera, et cetera. ... Huggy-huggy, touchy-touchy, feely-feely, kissy-kissy.
  Bless. Love.
**Jacintha** See how they struggle!
**Petronella** Forever doomed to toil away their lives in semi-darkness.
**Jacintha** Troglodytes in the theatre's cave.
**All** But not tonight!

*The Lights come up to their full working state during the following*

**Petronella** Strip away the illusion!
**Jacintha** Reveal the mysteries!
**Petronella** Expose the stage machinery!
**Wendy** Now this *is* what I call an alienation device!

*The stage crew become aware of their visibility. They stop what they are
doing, slowly freeze and face the audience. They seem rather pale and
uncertain. There is a moment*

**Wendy** Bit disappointing, actually, aren't they?
**All** Enough!

*The Lights go back to semi-darkness*

**Petronella** The magic of the theatre weaves its spell again.
**Wendy** Just a minute, just a minute! Aren't we having an interval?
**Petronella** Wendy, love, we've had the interval.
**Wendy** I mean a proper interval. Because I'll tell you this for nothing — I'm
  not going any further without a nice cup of tea and a Hobnob.

*And so saying, Wendy marches off*

*Jacintha and Petronella look at the audience and shrug*

**Petronella** ⎫
**Jacintha** ⎬ *(together)* Interval!

*They mince off*

# ACT II

*The front pews of the auditorium*

*The caption board is still in place*

*Darkness*

*The usherettes enter and grope their way about dramatically, their torches flashing*

**Jacintha** Once more the darkness.
**Petronella** Once more the reverent hush.
**Wendy** Let's just get on with it, shall we?

*Wendy changes the display to the caption: "16.40 hours. A Cough and a Spit"*

**All** 16.40 hours. *A Cough And A Spit.*

  *The usherettes exit. As they go :*

**Wendy** What a disgusting title.

*The Lights come up on the auditorium seats*

  *We should have the feeling of an audience having just left. Perhaps a few elderly people can just be discerned making their careful way out of the theatre*

*One figure remains alone in the second row. He is Werner Meister, a man in his early sixties. He sits slumped in his chair contemplating the floor. He was obviously once an impressive-looking figure but now he looks slightly shrunken and shabby in the large overcoat that, rather incongruously, he wears buttoned up to the neck. He has a large carrier bag. He looks as if he may have been crying*

*Benedict appears in the doorway at the top of the stairs. He has changed*
*into his everyday clothes and nurtures a beautifully developing black eye.*
*He looks around and registers Werner's presence with a mixture of delight*
*and apprehension. He moves down to him*

*Werner shows no sign of registering his presence*

**Benedict**  Mr Meister?

*No response*

   Um. Werner?

*At last, Werner looks up*

**Werner**  Ah.
**Benedict**  Yeah. It's me. It *is* you. I thought I heard you laughing.

*Werner turns a baleful stare on him*

   You should have come round.
**Werner**  I have never liked to do that. After a performance a cast needs time
   to ease back from their work back into ours. Outsiders intrude.
**Benedict**  Yeah. Right. I remember. (*He laughs*) It's great that you're ... it's
   great. You should have let me know you were coming, I could have ——
**Werner**  I did not know myself. I was passing and I thought I had not been
   in a theatre for some time.
**Benedict**  So you didn't come especially? To see ... um ... the play?
**Werner**  You were going to say something else, I think?
**Benedict**  I was going to say, you didn't come to see me.
**Werner**  And you know very well what I always tried to teach you at drama
   school.
**Benedict**  "Love the art in yourself, not yourself in art".
**Werner**  Just so. Remember, please.
**Benedict**  It's like being back in class again. Did you say you were just
   passing? You live here?
**Werner**  I have retired. To the provinces, as it happens.
**Benedict**  Good God ... You don't teach at the school?
**Werner**  As I say.
**Benedict**  I didn't know. I mean, I hadn't heard.
**Werner**  It was a spur of the moment decision.
**Benedict**  I can't imagine that place without you.
**Werner**  Then you are saying you have a very poor imagination and I know
   that not to be the case.

**Benedict** No, I mean — you were the inspiration ... we all said so. I mean — not just our year. Everybody. I'd never have got the Silver Medal without your ... well, everything, I suppose.

**Werner** You should have got the Gold Medal ——

**Benedict** But I didn't do enough voice work, I know.

**Werner** Also you smoked too much, I think.

**Benedict** I've given up. Six and a half months. My body is a temple. (*He holds his arms up dramatically and coughs slightly*)

**Werner** Is that the kind of thing I used to say?

**Benedict** All the time.

*Werner lapses into a silence*

You taught us that mantra. You know, the one we had to repeat at times when we — you know — doubted ourselves. Or our talent. I've forgotten it.

*Werner appears not to be listening*

What did you ... um. The play? I think it's a really interesting piece, I know I haven't got there yet, but I think there's a huge potential. What did you think?

**Werner** I thought it was — interesting.

**Benedict** You didn't like it.

**Werner** Did I say I didn't like it?

**Benedict** No, you're right. It's a pile of crap.

**Werner** It needs some work.

**Benedict** I only did it because, you know ... the rent ... but it is a pile of crap.

**Werner** No piece of work in the theatre is entirely worthless. Gems can always be found amongst the mud. But I must say in this piece it would take exceptional eyesight.

**Benedict** It's a very big pile of crap. Just as well I've only got a cough and a spit.

**Werner** To be entirely negative merely closes the door on creativity. Our work as actors is to open doors to allow the audience to marvel at the wonders within.

**Benedict** You said it. And that sort of — hits a lot of nails on the head as far as I'm concerned, in terms of, you know, what I've found since I've left college. Do you understand what I'm saying?

**Werner** I'm groping my way.

**Benedict** I mean, all the stuff we did at drama school, I mean, it was fantastic, I mean everything we did was worthwhile and good and full of sort of artistic ... you know ... And then you leave and you have to do well, crap, nearly all the time, I mean, not just crap plays like this but, you know, adverts, voice-overs ... and I wonder what that means, you know, about us as actors, about me as an actor, I mean — do you see what I'm getting at?

**Werner** How can one cope with playing *King Lear* on Saturday night and be evangelical about low-fat frankfurters at nine o'clock on Monday morning without compromising one's integrity?

**Benedict** Exactly! Exactly!

**Werner** Without losing sight of what we are as performers and artists.

**Benedict** Precisely! Precisely!

*There is a pause*

Well?

**Werner** The theatre is a difficult mistress.

**Benedict** Oh.

**Werner** All one can say is that one must treat the work, whatever it may be, with honesty and good creative intentions.

**Benedict** Yes, but, in the end it's a matter of ... I don't know ... it's a matter of ...

**Werner** Dignity?

**Benedict** Precisely! Precisely! I mean, it's degrading, as an actor being in ... as a human being, even, having to be stuff that's ... I mean, this sitcom that I'm in. Have you seen it? "There's Rue For You"?

**Werner** Hmmmm.

**Benedict** No, better, it's not me, thank God. But that advert on the telly — you know the one? For lettuce or salad cream or something? And there's this stupid pink rabbit that dances about and waves lettuces at the camera and goes "Yum yum?" I mean, I see that and I think — well, admittedly, I don't like salad cream personally — but I look at that rabbit and I think: there is an actor inside that suit. There is a brother of mine! The words of Shakespeare have passed over his lips! And now look at him! I mean, what's going through his mind in that furry suit as he waves the lettuce at the camera? What's he feeling? I mean, how does he look the crew in the eye? His family? Himself? I mean, it's degrading. Do you see what I mean?

**Werner** Suddenly you are very fluent.

**Benedict** There just seems to be a ... you know.

**Werner** Discrepancy.

**Benedict** Exactly! Precisely! But on the other hand, there's ... I mean, in this profession you're lucky to be working at all, whatever it is, so who am I to ... It's a funny old — um — business ...

*Werner reaches into his coat pocket and pulls out a pistol. It is very old but obviously still in working order. It is an impressive weapon, lovingly looked after. Not surprisingly, Benedict looks a little concerned*

**Werner** You remember the exercise with the pistol that we did at school?

**Benedict** (*relieved*) Truth from the barrel of a gun, yes.

**Werner** (*pointing the gun at his head*) You point the gun at your character's head — your character's, mind you, not yours, most important difference — and ——

**Benedict** — you have to, you know, sort of say what passes through your character's mind in the few seconds before death.

**Werner** I teach — taught — it to all my students. A great focusing exercise.

**Benedict** Bit of a relief. For a moment there when you pulled it out, I thought ——

**Werner** It is my father's pistol. Was. From the Great War. The First World War.

**Benedict** He was an actor, wasn't he?

**Werner** An actor-manager, yes. A great actor-manager. In Germany between the wars.

**Benedict** And he fled with Brecht when the Nazis came to power.

**Werner** You heard that story?

**Benedict** You told us that story.

**Werner** I have been thinking of my father a great deal recently. He taught me so much about acting that I still remember. He instilled me with such ideals about the art. I often wonder what he would make of his son?

**Benedict** What was it ... ? Something you told us ... about Chekhov and guns ...

**Werner** In Chekhov's hands a gun can make us laugh or cry. When Uncle Vanya fires and misses we laugh and cry in the same moment. In the end. Chekhov says that he is tired of plays that end with pistol shots.

**Benedict** But he also said ... something like, if a gun is pulled in a play, whenever, and the audience sees the gun and knows it's there, then it has to be fired.

*There is a pause. Werner puts the gun back into his pocket*

Why did you retire?

**Werner** I had taught enough.

**Benedict** You wanted to act again?

*Werner nods*

To see if you could still do it? That's what you always told us. The only way to learn, to improve, is to practise the craft.

**Werner** I told you that, yes.

**Benedict** Are you getting work? I mean, acting jobs? Mr Meister? Werner?

**Werner** Some ... interesting things have presented themselves.

**Benedict** That's good. That's great. I mean, you were a brilliant teacher, but it's great that you're out there again. Doing it. A working member of the profession. That's terrific.

*Zara and Hugo appear at either end of the top aisle. They glare at each other and then at Benedict. They exit, wordlessly*

Listen, I'm going to have to go, there's some people I have to see, in the cast, I mean, you know, talk to. Emotional problems, you know how it is. But it's been great seeing you again. Inspiring. It's sort of put me back in touch with what it's all about, reminded me why I wanted to come into the profession in the first place. And I'm going to make a resolution now. Because of ... From this moment on, I'm only ever going to do good work in the future. Worthwhile work. Noble. No crap. No sitcoms. To hell with the rent and the exposure. Good work — even if it is just a cough and a spit.

**Werner** That is a very laudable aim.

**Benedict** So. Bye, then, Mr Meister. Or Maestro. That's what we used to call you, by the way. The Maestro. We never told you but we did. Well ... (*He turns to leave but turns back*) Oh. I remember. The mantra. You know, the one you taught us? It was something like "We are the work. The work is us. The work we do defines what we are. In the end we are judged by the work we do." I won't forget it again.

*Benedict leaves*

*Werner sits there. He looks around the theatre. Then he stands, takes the gun out of his pocket and lays it down on the seat. He methodically undoes his overcoat. Underneath it he is wearing a pink furry rabbit suit. He reaches into the carrier bag and pulls out a ridiculous-looking rabbit head with large eyes and teeth. He puts on the rabbit head, picks up the gun from the seat and plods up the aisle. As he does so:*

*The usherettes enter, rather tentatively, as if they are waiting for something terrible to happen*

*Werner exits*

**Petronella** Unhappy man.
**Jacintha** The magic of theatre ——
**Petronella** —— has left his life.
**Jacintha** When that happens, when the light goes out ...
**Petronella** Only one thing left ...

*The usherettes crouch, their fingers stuck in their ears. They wait and wait,
but nothing happens. Gradually they remove their fingers and come to an
upright stance. They smile, weakly*

**Jacintha** Expectation.
**Petronella** Tension.
**Jacintha** Suspense.
**Petronella** ⎫
              ⎬ (*together*) The very life blood of theatre!
**Jacintha**  ⎭
**Wendy** To say nothing of anti-climax.

*Tanya appears. She is a very smart, highly organized-looking woman in
her early thirties, with a briefcase*

**Jacintha** See here the businesswoman.
**Petronella** The theatre's sponsor ...
**Jacintha** Cool, dispassionate, in control ——

*There is the most enormous explosion off stage*

Jesus Christ!

*The usherettes scream, become hysterical. Even Tanya looks a little concerned*

*The usherettes exit with lots of hugs and reassurances*

*Wendy re-enters and changes the caption. It reads: "17.15 hours. In Bed
with Mammon"*

**Wendy** 17.15 hours. *In Bed With* ... excuse me, I think I'm going to be
sick ...

*Tanya sits, picks up a programme for "Fecund" and reads it, not looking
happy. She looks at her watch*

*Estelle rushes in with her untidy sheaf of papers. She looks more harassed
and wayward than she did before*

**Estelle** Sorry about that; a small problem to be sorted out. Rabbit with a gun.
Showbiz. (*She laughs and shrugs, but it is an effort*)
**Tanya** Serious?

**Estelle**  Oh yes. I wouldn't joke about a thing like that. Oh, I see what you mean. No, he missed. Flesh wound. We've sent for the ambulance. That sort of thing doesn't happen very often, honestly. I wouldn't want you or your corporation getting the impression that we're always knee-deep in suicidal rabbits. Right. Well, hallo, umm, sorry, but in the panic I've forgotten ...

**Tanya**  Tanya.

**Estelle**  Right. Estelle. Sorry to be a bit late.

**Tanya**  That's all right. It's good of you to interface at such short notice.

**Estelle**  Yes ... Sorry we can't — interface — in my office but they're having to sort out the drains.

**Tanya**  That's no problem.

**Estelle**  You haven't tried working in there on a hot day! Sorry we can't meet in the coffee bar, but it closes between the matinée and the evening performance.

**Tanya**  Please, there's no need to keep apologizing.

**Estelle**  Sorry. Legacy of my years with British Rail. Sorry.

*Tanya smiles*

And it's taken me a little by surprise, your ringing and saying you wanted a meeting at such short notice.

**Tanya**  I do realize that in a sense we are both labouring under something of a difficulty. I've only recently taken over the company's Arts sponsorship brief from my predecessor. I understand that you're in a similar position here at the theatre, your predecessor having taken early retirement ...

**Estelle**  The ultimate early retirement ...

**Tanya**  I'm sorry?

**Estelle**  He died.

**Tanya**  Oh dear.

**Estelle**  Poor Mr Bissell. Stress-related.

**Tanya**  Estelle, I don't know what went on between our predecessors or what they had in mind when they put together the package, but I do know that they were both old men near the end of their careers ——

**Estelle**  Near the end of his life, in Mr Bissell's case ...

**Tanya**  Exactly. So when I came to look at the deal that had been made I'm sorry to have to tell you that I've uncovered a few little problems at your end that need resolving. (*She gets out a very impressive Filofax-cum-folder which is meticulously organized*)

*Estelle, after much patting of pockets and so on produces a scrappy piece of paper and a minute stub of pencil*

**Estelle** Oh dear. Well, I'm sure we can iron out any wrinkles without too
much trouble. What's the scale of the problem?
**Tanya** Almost the whole of your proposed entire season.

*Estelle looks at Tanya and gulps. During the following her eyes glaze and she
makes a small gargling noise*

I did say almost. We have no problem with the Agatha Christie or "Are
Those Your Trousers Or Mine?" Estelle?
**Estelle** (*coming out of her hiatus*) You're not? Oh, thank you, thank you.
We're desperately relying on that sponsorship.
**Tanya** You have to understand, Estelle, that we're just one division of a huge
international corporation with its head offices in Salt Lake City. (*She spots
something on the unseen stage, gets up and moves forward for a closer
look. She does not like what she sees*) We have to be very careful about what
we sponsor and what that sponsorship says about our corporate image. (*She
indicates the stage*) Is this what they call the set?

*Estelle nods*

Did somebody get killed?

*Estelle opens her mouth to explain but decides against it*

As I say, we have to be very careful about what we sponsor. There aren't
many rules, but they are golden. Rule One: always sponsor opera wherever
possible. Rule Two: whatever you sponsor, make sure that it's safe. To the
point of tedium, if possible. William Douglas Home's good. Early, but
definitely not late, Ayckbourn's just about OK. Any Agatha Christie's
better than both. Rule Three: if it's Shakespeare, make sure the director's
over sixty, desperate for work and belongs to the Garrick Club. So, in the
light of that, let's have a quick look at the season, shall we? Now then ...
*A Midsummer Night's Dream*
**Estelle** That should be all right, shouldn't it? Shakespeare? It's a nice play.
**Tanya** Hmm. But with these provisos:

*Estelle takes notes*

No mud, fairies only in the old-fashioned sense of the word, no nudity, no
trapezes.
**Estelle** (*scribbling away on her piece of paper*) Trapezes ... right ...
**Tanya** *Showboat* ... oh, dear.

**Estelle**  What's wrong?

**Tanya**  All those slaves. Toting the bales of cotton. Many of Pharmacorp's leading brands are made almost exclusively of cotton. Having all of these oppressed people doing a lot of heavy toting for very little money rather casts Pharmacorp in the light of a cruel exploiter of underwaged workers. Which, of course, we are, but the last thing we want is to have it celebrated on a public stage. But these are all incidentals. Our real problem is this ... (*She holds the "Fecund" programme with some distaste at arm's length*)

**Estelle**  "Fecund"?

**Tanya**  "Fecund". A new play. Oh. I forgot to mention Rule Four: never, never, never sponsor new work by people who are still breathing. It's simply asking for trouble. So let's have a little think about "Fecund", shall we? In this play, a woman gives birth. That's good. But ...

**Estelle**  There's always a "but", isn't there?

**Tanya**  The woman is in labour for the whole of the play. It is a long birth. It is painful. It is bloody. She contemplates the virtues of abortion at some length.

**Estelle**  Yes? And?

**Tanya**  Do you know what Pharmacorp's major product line is, Estelle?

*Estelle thinks. She shakes her head*

Nappies. The Fluffidump fully absorbent disposable nappy.

**Estelle**  Yes! I've seen your adverts on television. All those little babies dancing ... Oh ...

**Tanya**  I think you're beginning to see our problem with "Fecund".

**Estelle**  Oh God.

**Tanya**  Every word in that play and everything that happens violates every clause of Pharmacorp's Sponsorship Charter. So what I'm proposing is a rewrite.

**Estelle**  A rewrite?

**Tanya**  I'm just flagging up the notion that it could be rewritten in such a way that it reinforced Pharmacorp's corporate identity.

**Estelle**  Yes, but — it's Roland, you see? Roland Luckett.

**Tanya**  The author.

**Estelle**  The playwright, yes. You don't know what playwrights are like. They shout. They wave their arms about a lot. They press against you with their jumbo sausages. They are just very, very odd people. So I don't think he'd be willing to ——

**Tanya**  Perhaps if I interfaced with him?

**Estelle**  You mean meet him? Well, you could try. I'll just ——

*Wendy enters with an armful of bandages and a first aid kit which are obviously destined for Werner off stage. She rushes across the back of the auditorium*

Wendy? Could you just see if Mr Luckett's backstage and if he is ask him to join us out here? Thank you.

*Wendy dithers for a moment, torn between Werner and her new instructions, but eventually she dashes off the way she arrived*

He shouldn't be a minute.

**Tanya** Good. Because we have no time to waste if we're to get things cleaned up in time for Aaron Zoffany the Third's visit and reception.

**Estelle** I'm sorry?

**Tanya** Aaron Zoffany the Third. Pharmacorp's International Corporate Chairman.

**Estelle** I'm sorry ...

**Tanya** (*rapturously*) Grandson of Aaron Zoffany the First, the Founder of Pharmacorp. He's flying in from Salt Lake City in the company's private jet. For tonight's performance. It's a great honour. The first time he'll have been seen in public outside Utah for seven years, since he went into spiritual retreat with Cherry and Buzz.

**Estelle** Cherry and Buzz?

**Tanya** His favourite two handmaidens. We'd call them wives.

**Estelle** Two wives?

**Tanya** He's a fanatical Mormon.

**Estelle** And he's coming here tonight?

**Tanya** He'll be landing at seven and coming straight from the airport. It's quite a coup for Pharmacorp UK. You did get my fax last week?

*Estelle looks aghast but manages to nod her head vigorously*

(*Reverently*) The food at the reception will, of course, be vegan and Mr Zoffany Three insists that the auditorium be completely sterile. He's very — particular about germs. That is in hand?

*Once again, Estelle manages a nod*

**Tanya** Excellent.

*Roland enters. He is now totally sober but nervy and anxious*

Is this Mr Luckett?

*Tanya approaches Roland; he looks even more anxious*

Tanya Steele, Mr Luckett. Pharmacorp.

**Roland** Don't believe a word that woman says to you! You don't frighten me! I am a perfectly normal, healthy man in his prime! You represent no threat to me or my sexuality!

**Tanya** I'm very glad to hear it, Mr Luckett. Roland. (*She gives a look to Estelle*)

*Estelle shrugs in an "I told you so" way*

Well, Roland, shall we go somewhere and interface? (*She heads for the exit*)

**Roland** Interface? Interface? Inter — I'm beginning to feel better already. With the very greatest of pleasure, Tanya, was it? (*To himself*) And to think I'd written today off ...

*Tanya exits; Roland heads after her*

I have a very comfortable room in a nearby local hotel in which I think things may be looking up ...

*Roland exits*

*Estelle sits there, her face a mixture of suppressed panic and distress. She riffles through her papers and pulls out the very crumpled, distinctively coloured fax on which she blew her nose earlier on. It is obviously Tanya's fax. She lets out an ear-piercing wail and screams out of the auditorium*

*Estelle exits*

*The Lights fade to Black-out*

*Music. The Lights come up on the auditorium*

*Wendy enters, in a rush, with a little rubbish bag. She goes down the rows of seats, pushing them up and picking up bits of litter, etc. She picks up a lettuce leaf, looks at it quizzically, puts it in her little bag. A disaster occurs; she loses a contact lens*

**Wendy** Oh. (*She bends down to pick the contact lens up; the other one falls out*) Oh.

*Lionel Heap and his wife, June, appear at the top of the aisle. Lionel is in his forties, a straightforward, unimaginative man used to getting his own way. June is about the same age, a mousey, anonymous woman, well used to Lionel getting his own way. Lionel carries a stop-watch and a small cooler bag and June a large carry-all, a handbag and a copy of the "Fecund" programme*

*Wendy panics and moves her feet. There is a crunching noise*

**Wendy** Oh. Um. (*Desperate, she squints at the rows of seats in front of her and tries to memorize the numbers*) D11, 12, 13, 14. C11, 12, 13, 14. B11, 12, 13, 14. A11, 12, 13, 14. AA11, 12, 13, 14. (*She runs over them again, under her breath, rapidly, then nods approvingly to confirm that they have gone in, which they haven't. She just about manages to locate Lionel and June, then runs up the aisle to them, feeling her way*) Can I help you at all?
**Lionel** I should think so. Do you know how long we've ——
**Wendy** (*turning around and scuttling back down the aisle*) Excuse me. Shan't be a moment ...

*Lionel is not amused. He sets his stop-watch working*

*Wendy arrives at the front, changes the caption and peers at it, short-sightedly*

Slide/caption: *"19.15 hours. Bums on Seats"*

**Wendy** (*to the audience*) I don't know why we've bothered with all this. Anyone can read that, surely? Nineteen fifteen hours. *Mums On Heat.* (*She feels her way back up the aisle*) Sorry about that. May I show you to your seat at all?
**Lionel** Just one moment. We have been waiting ...

*Estelle enters, beating them to it. She is in something of a state*

**Estelle** Wendy! Wendy!

*Wendy peers about her and locates Estelle. She feels her way towards her*

What's the matter with you?
**Wendy** I've lost both my contact ——
**Estelle** Never mind that. We haven't got time. Do you know any shops that sell vegan food? In fact, do you know what vegan food is?
**Wendy** Something to do with milk, I think.
**Estelle** Tesco's? Would they have a vegan counter?
**Wendy** Waitrose, more likely.
**Estelle** Right. Hold the fort. And, um, disinfect. The auditorium.
**Wendy** Right.
**Estelle** Good.
**Wendy** Why? (*She heads back up the aisle*)

*Tanya appears. She has a mobile phone at her ear and looks surprisingly dishevelled*

**Tanya** His plane's just landed. It's taxiing. Everything all right your end?
**Estelle** Yes, yes. Excuse me. Oh. How was Roland? Mr Luckett?
**Tanya** *(fractionally losing her cool for the first time)* I don't begin to see what that has to do with you.

*Tanya and Estelle go off in different directions, Tanya coolly, Estelle rather less so*

*Wendy finally makes it to Lionel and June. Lionel clicks off his stopwatch*

**Lionel** *(to June)* One minute, seventeen seconds.
**Wendy** I beg your pardon?
**Lionel** *(to June)* Write it down. Write it down in the book.

*June writes in the small notebook that she has with her*

One minute, seventeen seconds between our arriving at this point and being greeted by our usherette. Not on, is it?
**Wendy** Well, we are rather ——
**Lionel** Not in view of the amount of subsidy the good people of this town pour into the place.
**June** Lionel ...
**Lionel** Be quiet, June. *(To Wendy)* I am Councillor Lionel Heap. You may have seen my picture in the local newspaper.
**Wendy** No, sorry.
**Lionel** I represent the Labour Party on the Leisure and Amenities Committee, and may therefore be said to technically be your employer. And, as your employer, I am bound to say that being kept waiting one minute and seventeen seconds is not good enough.
**June** Lionel, please, it's my birthday ...
**Lionel** Be quiet, June.
**Wendy** Well, all I can do is to apologize on behalf of all of us here at the Theatre Royal, from the Artistic Director down to the theatre cat and ask for your tickets.
**Lionel** Tickets, June.

*June puts down her notebook and carry-all and rummages around in her handbag*

**Lionel** Come on, come on.
**June** ... had them here somewhere ...

**Lionel**  Bob give me strength. And she wonders why I never bring her to the theatre.

**June**  Here they ——

**Lionel**  Give them to the girl, then. That's the idea. You give them to the girl. That's what she's here for. That's why we pay her out of our hard-earned taxes.

**June**  (*handing over the tickets, almost indistinguishably*)  It's B13 and ...

**Wendy**  (*peering hard at the tickets*)  Just a minute, just a minute, please ...

**June**  Thank you.

**Lionel**  What are you saying thank you for?

**June**  (*to Wendy*)  Just being polite.

*Wendy is not listening*

**Lionel**  No, my dear. She says thank you to you. At these prices she should go down on her knees in gratitude.

**Wendy** (*pointedly*)  Thank you. (*She peers at the ticket again*) A13 and A14.

**June**  No ... It's B13 and ——

**Wendy**  Thank you. Just follow me. Thank you.

*Lionel follows Wendy, leaving June dithering at the top of the aisle*

**Lionel**  (*to June*)  Come on, then! Come on! You heard the girl! Is this them?

**Wendy**  Thank you. A13 and A14, yes. Thank you.

**Lionel**  About time, too. Sit down, June.

**Wendy**  (*to Lionel, indicating his cooler bag*)  Thank you. May I take that from you, sir?

**Lionel**  You may not.

**Wendy**  Right, sir. Thank you. And may I take this chance to wish you a long and painful death in excruciating circumstances as a result of your experience in the theatre tonight? Thank you. (*She moves off. During the following, she goes down on her knees, trying to find and piece together her contact lenses*)

*Wendy's comments take a few seconds to percolate Lionel's consciousness. He clicks his stopwatch again*

**Lionel**  Three minutes, thirty seven seconds. What did she say?

**June**  Who?

**Lionel**  The girl.

**June**  I didn't hear. Nice seats, aren't they, Lionel? They've put us in the front row. (*She pulls at Lionel's sleeve*)

**Lionel**  Don't pull at my sleeve, June.

**June**  They are nice seats, aren't they?

**Lionel** If one wants to get a crick in the neck and be spat at by actors with unmentionable diseases. In fact, I may ask to be moved.

**June** Lionel? Why couldn't we have a drink in the bar?

**Lionel** Did you see the price of a light ale? Scandalous. I shall be having words at the next Leisure and Amenities. I've always held the view that the theatre is an expensive, over subsidized upper-middle-class beanfeast, and nothing I have seen so far this evening changes my view.

**June** It is my birthday treat, Lionel.

**Lionel** Fear not. As ever, I have come prepared. (*He opens his cooler bag and takes out a bottle of light ale and a bottle of Cinzano*) Can I offer you a sweet Cinzano, June?

**June** Are we allowed? In here?

**Lionel** My dear woman, as you never seem to appreciate, I am on the Council. I have some sway in this place. Drink up and be of good heart. Cheers. Is that the programme?

**June** Yes.

**Lionel** (*grabbing the programme from her*) How much did this cost?

**June** One pound fifty.

**Lionel** Good heavens, woman, are you under the impression we're made of money. Bob knows the tickets cost enough.

**June** It's my birthday treat, Lionel. And I paid for it out of my own money.

**Lionel** You have no money, June. Your money is my money. And I'm well aware it's your birthday treat. I'm here, aren't I? (*He reads the programme*) Thank Bob for that! I thought for one terrible moment you'd let me in for another one man show. I hate one man shows. You pay fourteen pounds fifty for a ticket and get one person droning on for the whole evening. Do you call that value for money? Because I don't. How many in this one? (*He counts*)

*There is a loud, fruity laugh from Gerald Bliss Hart, off stage*

(*Freezing*) Oh no.

**June** What is it, Lionel?

**Lionel** Pray to Bob that isn't who I think it is.

*Gerald and Marcia appear at the top of the aisle. Gerald is a large, florid, very well-dressed man in his early fifties. Marcia is younger, expensively dressed and made-up, carrying a handbag. Gerald is turning back to finish a conversation with somebody outside*

*Wendy sets off to greet the Bliss Harts; she moves slowly up the aisle*

**Gerald** That's right! That's right! And you can tell him I jolly well said so! Ha, ha, ha!

**Lionel**  Oh, ruddy hell it is! Gerald Bliss Hart.

**Gerald**  *Ciao, amigo.* See you at the next Lodge!

**Lionel**  Leader of the Conservative mob on the council. Hide behind the programme! Hide! Perhaps he won't ...

**Gerald**  Is this a Heap I see before me?

**Marcia**  Gerald ...

**Lionel**  Oh Bob — don't listen to him, June.

**Gerald**  It is! It's a socialist Heap! Old Stinky Heap! And I thought that smell was the drains!

**Marcia**  Really, Gerald, this evening is proving ghastly enough as it is. You've over-indulged again ——

**Lionel**  Just ignore him, June.

**Gerald**  Only joking. Comrade Heap.

**Marcia**  — despite what the doctor told you ...

**Gerald**  Only joking. Got a sense of humour, haven't you, Stinky?

**Lionel**  Don't rise to the bait, June.

**Gerald**  Must have a sense of humour, mustn't he, darling — belonging to the Labour Party! Ha, ha, ha!

**Lionel**  (*shouting*) Oh — boil your head, Bliss Hart!

**Gerald**  Now, now — temper, temper! You're not with the comrades now! Ha, ha, ha.

**Marcia**  Really Gerald, do you have to be so juvenile?

*Wendy reaches Gerald and Marcia at the top of the aisle*

**Wendy**  Good-evening, sir. Madam.

**Gerald**  Good-evening, yourself, my dear. And what delights have you got for us this evening?

**Marcia**  And please don't start flirting with the staff.

**Gerald**  Opera, is it?

**Marcia**  You know perfectly well it isn't.

**Gerald**  I love a bit of opera. Nice tunes with a nap in between.

**Wendy**  May I see your tickets, please, sir?

**Gerald**  Tickets, tickets, now who was getting the ——

**Marcia**  You were, Gerald.

**Gerald**  Was I?

**Marcia**  I offered but as usual you had to be in charge of everything, so you got them.

**Gerald**  Did I? Well, I'll tell you what, my dear, I seem to have mislaid them. Put them on the dressing table and forgotten them.

**Marcia**  Honestly ...

**Gerald**  But I remember the seat numbers perfectly. They're the seats we always have.

**Wendy** I have to see the tickets, sir. I'm not authorized to take any other action.

**Gerald** Well, then, perhaps you could direct me to your superior who is authorized? Tell him that Gerald Bliss Hart, the Leader of the Council, and his wife, Marcia, are being kept waiting. The Leader of the Council that nods through a very substantial subsidy for this place every year? Perhaps you'd like to do that, my dear?

**Wendy** (*swallowing hard*) In view of the circumstances, sir, perhaps we at the Theatre Royal can be a little more flexible.

**Gerald** Jolly good. I thought you'd see it my way, my dear.

**Wendy** What seats were they, sir?

**Gerald** Our usual. A13 and A14.

**Wendy** Very good, sir. If you'd follow me?

**Marcia** Well done, Gerald. There are times when I remember why I married you. (*Under her breath*) Almost.

*Halfway down the aisle Wendy realizes that Lionel and June are sitting in A13 and A14*

**Wendy** Oh. Umm — actually, there does seem to have been a misunderstanding. Councillor Heap and his wife ——

**Gerald** Are sitting in our seats? Oh dear. Are you sitting in our seats, Stinky? You're going to have to shift, old son.

**Lionel** Not a chance.

**June** Let's not cause a fuss, Lionel.

**Lionel** You stay put, do you hear?

**Gerald** This your better half, poor woman?

*During the following Wendy resumes the hunt in the front rows for her contact lenses*

**June** (*virtually curtsying*) June Heap, how d'you do.

**Lionel** Don't bow and scrape! What are you bowing and scraping for?

**Gerald** This is Marcia.

**June** How d'you do.

**Lionel** June! Just because he's the Leader of the Council doesn't mean ——

**Marcia** Delighted.

**Wendy** Lovely. Very nice. Well, now we've got the formalities over — you're going to have to shift.

**Lionel** You needn't think you can come in here and thrown your weight about just because you've got a double-barrelled name.

**Wendy** Have you got tickets?

**Lionel** Of course we've got tickets. June! Tickets!

**June** Oh yes ... now then, let me see ... had them here somewhere ——
**Lionel** For Pete's sake, June, will you find those ——
**June** — gave them to the girl — got them back from the girl — put them ——
**Gerald** Because if you haven't got tickets you'll have to move. In fact, that's dishonest. I ought to have a word with the usherette to get you thrown out.

*Wendy pops up from behind the first row at the mention of her office*

*Gerald is mildly surprised*

*Wendy pops down again, still looking for her shattered lenses*

**Marcia** Gerald, really ...
**June** Oh, Lionel ...
**Lionel** Let's see your tickets, then!
**Gerald** What's that? Oh, tickets, well, the fact is we left them at home ...
**Lionel** You didn't even buy any tickets. I've heard about you, chum, don't worry.
**Gerald** What are you implying, you oik?
**Lionel** Throwing your weight around. Insisting on free tickets. Not expecting to pay for anything.
**Gerald** I pay my way and I resent you implying that I don't.
**Marcia** (*to June*) They're obviously going to be at this all evening.
**Lionel** We on our side know what you lot are up to, don't you worry.
**Marcia** (*to June*) Why don't we go and powder our noses?
**Gerald** What do you mean by that?
**June** (*to Marcia*) Me?
**Lionel** All your little magic handshakes and treating this theatre as though it's your own private little preserve ...
**Gerald** That's an outrageous suggestion!

*June and Marcia move up the aisle to the Ladies. Marcia talks as they walk. June bows and scrapes along behind her*

**Marcia** This council stuff's so dreary, isn't it?
**June** Lionel never tells. He says I wouldn't understand.
**Marcia** You've heard of golf widows? I'm a council zombie. And with Gerald, if it's not the council, it's bloody opera.
**June** I love opera myself.
**Marcia** Really? How extraordinary.

*Marcia sweeps into the Ladies*

**June** Oh, yes. I watch her every afternoon. Did you know she had a terrible weight problem ... ?

*June disappears into the Ladies*

*Lionel and Gerald are still sniping*

**Lionel** Do you know, are you fully aware of how many thousands of pounds' worth of subsidy the Council pours into this place every year?

**Gerald** Of course I am, you bloody fool. I authorize it.

**Lionel** My point exactly! And what do we get? Operas, operas and more operas, just so you and your elitist chums can come and show off by nodding your head in time to the music and moving your lips as though you know the words. And then you come out for champagne and smoked salmon sandwiches, which is what it's really all about. You might as well just stay in the bar and turn the record player on.

**Gerald** Rubbish. We have the occasional ballet.

**Lionel** And I know who pays for it! Me and my kind, through our taxes.

**Wendy** (*popping up from behind her row, very quietly*) True, true.

**Gerald** You're talking through your fundament.

**Lionel** What we need is to open up this place to the people.

**Gerald** What people?

**Wendy** Good question.

**Lionel** (*floundering slightly*) The people. In general. The community.

**Wendy** Which community?

**Lionel** I beg your pardon?

**Wendy** Which community?

**Gerald** Exactly!

**Lionel** (*to Wendy*) You keep out of this! What's this got to do with you anyway? You're only an usherette!

**Wendy** I'm a member of the community.

**Lionel** What?

**Wendy** (*indignantly*) I am a member of the community!

*Tanya enters, at the top of the aisle, mobile phone at her ear*

**Tanya** Usherette? Usherette!

*Wendy feels her way up the aisle to meet Tanya*

(*To Wendy*) The stretch limo's on its way from the airport. Oh, and another piece of news. I've just been speaking to Buzz. Apparently, whenever Mr Zoffany the Third goes to a public performance, he always, always sits in the same numbered seat.

**Wendy** Don't tell me. Let me guess.

**Tanya** It's a family superstition. A vision his grandfather had in the Nevada desert.

**Wendy** Z39, is it?
**Tanya** A13.
**Wendy** Surprise, surprise.
**Tanya** See to it, will you? And has this place been disinfected, as I asked?

*Wendy bristles, but decides to bite the bullet. She sighs and moves half-heartedly down to Gerald and company and begins to break the news*

*During the following, Tanya turns to exit. As she does so:*

*Roland appears. He is totally sober and very smug and confident*

*Roland smiles at Tanya. She glares back. As they pass he pats her on the bottom. She wheels round furiously but is too late. Roland sits in a seat at the back, where he sits surveying his world*

*Tanya exits*

**Wendy** (*to Lionel*) I'm sorry, sir — actually, I'm not sorry at all, I'm just saying that because my lowly job demands it — but I'm going to have to ask you to move, to make way for the third Mr Zoffany — I don't know what's happened to the other two — who is apparently completely off his trolley as a result of a collision his grandmother had in the Mojave desert. And if you can make any sense of that you're a better woman than I am. Thank you.

*Wendy, having done her duty, moves back to the top of the aisle and exits, seeking disinfectant*

**Gerald** (*to Lionel*) Now surely to God you'll move, man?
**Lionel** For some American religious zillionaire? Not likely.
**Gerald** This is one of the richest and most important men in the US of A! The head of one of the largest corporations in the free world! A massive employer of local labour! Have you any idea of the sweeteners we as a council had to offer Pharmacorp to get them to base their European operation here?
**Lionel** Sweeteners? Just as we on our side have always suspected! Bribery, corruption and sleaze. The Holy Trinity of the Tory Party. And just what did you get in return, my friend?

*Wendy returns, clutching a large industrial-sized sprayer of disinfectant*

**Gerald** Let me point out a few facts of commercial life to you, Heap ...

*Gerald moves into June's seat next to Lionel and whispers furiously in his ear. Wendy tries a tentative squirt of her disinfectant, just behind Roland's seat. At the same moment:*

*Marcia comes out of the Ladies spraying herself with expensive perfume. She moves past Roland*

**Roland** (*sniffing appreciatively*) Ah, Chanel Number Five! Simply but so lingeringly erotic! A classic!

*Wendy looks at her disinfectant bottle quizzically and shrugs*

**Marcia** I beg your ... don't I recognize you?
**Roland** Possibly. I am a playwright.
**Marcia** A writer?

*Roland shrugs modestly. A change seems to come over Marcia. She becomes more predatory. She slides into the seat next to Roland*

A real writer? Yes — I've seen your photograph somewhere ...
**Roland** Outside the theatre perhaps?
**Marcia** No, no. Somewhere else. On the back of a book. I can't remember the title. I think it had a brown cover ... Anyway ... a writer. I've always been fascinated by writers. You won't believe this, but my degree was in English.
**Roland** I believe it. I see sensitivity ingrained in every one of your lovely features.
**Marcia** So I've always loved and adored creative artists. Painters, sculptors, concert pianists ... but my real passion has always been writers, creative writers, who can touch me at the very living centre of my being ... I have to confess — I hope you don't mind — I find them aphrodisiac.

*Roland whimpers*

**Gerald** ... so it's simple, Heap. You get your arse out of that seat or I'll ...

*Gerald grabs Lionel by the lapel. Lionel resists. It develops into a fuzzy, unresolved struggle between two out-of-condition middle-aged men. Lionel just about manages to keep his seat on the chair*

*Roland starts to get a bit physical with Marcia*

**Roland** I have a very comfortable room with a small fridge in a nearby local hotel. Come with me there, now!

**Marcia**  Yes, yes! Oh yes!
**Roland**  There is a God! There is a God!

*Estelle enters, weighed down with Waitrose carrier bags*

**Estelle** (*to Wendy*) Eight different kinds of cheese, fromage frais, and full fat
ice cream for afters.
**Wendy** (*indicating her pump*) Ibcol.

*Estelle nods, then notices the wrestling figures in the front and back rows*

**Estelle**  What's going on here? (*To Marcia and Roland*) Excuse me. This is
a theatre. We don't allow passion ...

*Marcia tears herself away from Roland and stares at Estelle*

**Marcia**  Estelle Nettlebank!
**Roland**  What? What?
**Estelle** (*after a moment, agog*)  Miss Thruxton!
**Roland**  Aaaaagh!
**Gerald** (*simultaneously*)  Aaaagh!
**Roland**  You're Miss Thruxton?
**Gerald**  My chest! Pains in my chest!
**Marcia**  My maiden name.
**Roland**  *The* Miss Thruxton?
**Marcia**  Gerald! Oh my God! What's wrong with Gerald?
**Gerald**  Pains in my arm!
**Marcia**  We're coming! My darling! We're coming!
**Roland**  If only that were true. (*He looks tragically at his lap*)
**Lionel** (*getting up from his seat*)  I never touched him!
**Marcia** (*guiding Gerald into Lionel's seat*)  It's his heart. I told him to lose
weight! The stupid, stubborn man! The doctors warned him time and time
again. Gerald, oh Gerald!

*Wendy examines Gerald*

*Disenchanted and detumesced, Roland picks up June's Cinzano bottle and
begins to drink from it. He wanders away to another part of the stalls, the
bottle to his lips*

**Estelle**  Wendy, ambulance!
**Wendy**  Too late, I'm afraid.
**Estelle**  What did you say?
**Wendy** (*virtually shouting*)  It's too late! He's ——

*Tanya arrives at the top of the stairs from the foyer. She is even more dishevelled and is clutching a large roll of industrial cleaning paper, which she is laying on the ground in front of the great man*

**Tanya** — arrived. He's on his way up. Are we all ready? (*She surveys the chaos in front of her. Finally, she eventually loses her cool completely*) Oh God! Who's that sitting in A13? In his seat! (*To Wendy*) I thought I told you ... oh God ... He is here! Aaron Zoffany the Third is here! (*She waves the company to their places and prostrates in front of her idol, unrolling the paper so that he may walk on it*)

*Aaron Zoffany The Third enters. If casting permits, it would be nice if he had a strange entourage consisting of goths in black leather, ex-hippies and smart-suited business people. Aaron Zoffany is even weirder-looking than his cohorts. He/she is a sort of combination of Howard Hughes and Michael Jackson, a thin, frail, highly androgynous creature of indeterminate age with very long, wispy hair and dark glasses. Possibly this is topped off with a Stetson. He wears an all-in-one sterile jumpsuit of a strange shiny material designed to keep out germs. He is barefooted. He may even breathe through a mask. He treads carefully on the paper being laid in front of him*

*Estelle indicates to Wendy that she should begin spraying. Wendy pumps up her sprayer and does so, liberally, walking in front of the Zoffany party*

*Aaron passes the door of the Ladies'. As he does so:*

*The door opens and June comes out, unawares. She is grotesquely and amateurishly made-up, obviously under Marcia's influence. She falls naturally in step with Aaron and steps carefully on the paper, smiling vacantly up at him*

*Aaron and June move down the aisle like a hideously weird wedding party approaching the altar. They reach the front row where Gerald is slumped in A13. Estelle indicates that Wendy should give him an extra squirt of disinfectant, which she does. Aaron clears his throat*

**Lionel** (*hissing*) June! Come away from that creature!
**Tanya** I, Tanya, newly elevated third handmaiden of Aaron Zoffany the Third, declare unto you that he is about to speak!

*Everyone waits, expectantly. Aaron leans into the dead Gerald and taps his shoulder. Gerald's head lolls back. Aaron flinches momentarily and turns to see June smiling up at him. He flinches again and turns back to Gerald. He clears his throat again*

**Aaron** (*in a cracked, whispery voice*) Excuse me, sir. I believe you're sitting in my seat.

*There is a silence. Tanya applauds frantically. June joins in. Everybody else stands, mystified.*

*The "houselights" dim, the "curtain" rises and Zara's voice is heard ringing out, as from the stage*

**Zara** (*off*) Ah! The pain! The pain! The terrible, unbearable pain!

*The figures stand frozen, staring transfixedly at the stage. Then chaos breaks out again with characters pursuing each other, drinking, fornicating*

*The Lights fade to black on a scene reminiscent of the last days of the Roman Empire*

   *All the cast — except Estelle — exits*

*The Lights come up on the auditorium. It is much later*

*The auditorium is in semi-darkness, the houselights having been turned off and the cleaning lights put on*

*Estelle sits alone, a pad on her knees, and a pen in hand*

   *Wendy appears in her everyday clothes, obviously on her way home. She starts slightly when she sees Estelle*

**Wendy** Oh, Miss Nettlebank. I didn't expect ... all on your ownsome?
**Estelle** That's right, Wendy.
**Wendy** I like to do that. You know, come in here when everyone's gone and ... Mr Bissell — your predecessor — he used to come and sit in here like this. It used to move him, I could tell, because quite often he was in tears. I don't know. There's just something about a theatre, isn't there?
**Estelle** There certainly is, Wendy. There certainly is.
**Wendy** Been a bit of a day, really. All round.
**Estelle** Yes.
**Wendy** That's what I love about it. I mean, we all moan, well, I mean, they don't, but I do — but every day's something different, isn't it? The people,

the plays, the lights — even the smell. Everything. It's just — magic, I think.
**Estelle**  Yes.
**Wendy**  The magic of theatre.
**Estelle**  Yes.
**Wendy**  Oh, well. Another day tomorrow.
**Estelle**  Yes.
**Wendy**  I'll say good-night, then.

*But there is no response from Estelle*

Good-night, then.

*Wendy goes*

*Estelle is left on her own. She sighs deeply, comes out of her reverie, looks at her pad and considers what she has written so far*

**Estelle**  "The Personnel Department, British Rail, Network South East. Dear Sir, I am applying for the position of——(*she starts to write*) — anything, really. Customer complaints clerk, station announcer, anything. I already have considerable experience of working in both British Rail as well as two weeks' experience of working in the theatre ... " (*She stops and considers, then crosses out the last few words*) "I already have considerable experience of working in British Rail, as well as two weeks' Psychiatric Work Experience as part of a Care In The Community project. I enclose my CV and hope that you will please, please be able to consider me because, to be frank, I am desperate ..."

*The Lights fade. Music swells*

CURTAIN

# FURNITURE AND PROPERTY LIST

## ACT I

*On stage*:     Operating table. *On it*: bloodied white sheet, bloodied baby doll
Other delivery room furniture and fittings
Seats
Notice-board or screen
Captions

*Off stage*:     Torch (**Wendy**)
Torch (**Petronella**)
Torch (**Jacintha**)
Untidy sheaf of papers with one distinctively coloured sheet(**Estelle**)
Polystyrene cup of coffee, cigarette (**Mo**)
*Daily Telegraph* (**Zara**)
Briefcase. *In it*: calculator, papers, pen, "Fecund" programme (**Hugo**)
Small flash camera (**Wendy**)
Wheelchair (**Zara**)

*Personal*:     **Estelle**: watch
**Wendy**: handkerchief
**Zara**: handbag containing pen, fashionable glasses, untidy wodge of
    receipts, condom
**Petronella**: "Fecund" programme
**Jacintha**: "Fecund" programme
**Benedict**: blood capsule

During set change sequence pp. 34-36:

*Strike*:     Delivery room set and hospital equipment

*Set*:     Auditorium setting
Theatre pews
"Fecund" programme for **Tanya**
Rubbish, including a lettuce leaf

## ACT II

*Off stage*:     Torch (**Wendy**)
Torch (**Petronella**)
Torch (**Jacintha**)

Large carrier bag containing rabbit costume head (**Werner**)
Briefcase (**Tanya**)
Untidy sheaf of papers (**Estelle**)
Bandages, first aid kit (**Wendy**)
Little rubbish bag (**Wendy**)
Small cooler bag (**Lionel**)
Large carry-all (**June**)
Mobile phone (**Tanya**)
Industrial-sized disinfectant spray (**Wendy**)

*Personal*:    Pistol (**Werner**)
Scrappy piece of paper, minute stub of pencil (**Estelle**)
Handbag containing small notebook, tickets; "Fecund" programme
(**June**)
Handbag containing perfume spray (**Marcia**)

# LIGHTING PLOT

Practical fittings required: nil
Two interiors. A stage, an auditorium

ACT I

*To open*: Semi-darkness

| *Cue* 12 | **Wendy**: "Thank God for that."<br>*Lighting change* | (Page 31) |
|---|---|---|
| *Cue* 13 | **Hugo** stiffens and freezes<br>*"Strange" lighting effect* | (Page 32) |
| *Cue* 14 | Blurred voice is heard for second time<br>*Slowly return lights to Cue 8 setting* | (Page 33) |
| *Cue* 15 | **Hugo**: "It's a boy!"<br>*"Curtain down" effect* | (Page 34) |
| *Cue* 16 | The actors line up for the curtain call<br>*"Curtain up" effect* | (Page 34) |
| *Cue* 17 | **Hugo** and **Zara** rejoin the company line; bow<br>*"Curtain down" effect* | (Page 34) |
| *Cue* 18 | **Benedict** and **Hugo** stagger off<br>*Return lights to opening setting* | (Page 34) |
| *Cue* 19 | **All**: "But not tonight!"<br>*Bring up lights to full working state* | (Page 36) |
| *Cue* 20 | **All**: "Enough!"<br>*Return lights to opening setting* | (Page 36) |

## ACT II

*To open*: Darkness

| *Cue* 21 | **Wendy**: "What a disgusting title."<br>*Bring up general lighting* | (Page 37) |
|---|---|---|
| *Cue* 22 | **Estelle** exits<br>*Fade lights to black-out* | (Page 48) |
| *Cue* 23 | Music<br>*Bring up lights on auditorium* | (Page 48) |
| *Cue* 24 | **Tanya** and **June** applaud<br>*Dim "house lights"; "curtain up" effect* | (Page 61) |
| *Cue* 25 | Chaos breaks out<br>*Fade lights to black-out* | (Page 61) |
| *Cue* 26 | All the cast except **Estelle** exits<br>*Bring up "cleaning lights"* | (Page 61) |
| *Cue* 27 | **Estelle**: "I am desperate ..."<br>*Fade lights to black-out* | (Page 62) |

# EFFECTS PLOT

## ACT I